Computer
Basics

Other Publications:
AMERICAN COUNTRY
VOYAGE THROUGH THE UNIVERSE
THE THIRD REICH
THE TIME-LIFE GARDENER'S GUIDE
MYSTERIES OF THE UNKNOWN
TIME FRAME
FIX IT YOURSELF
FITNESS, HEALTH & NUTRITION
SUCCESSFUL PARENTING
HEALTHY HOME COOKING
LIBRARY OF NATIONS
THE ENCHANTED WORLD
THE KODAK LIBRARY OF CREATIVE PHOTOGRAPHY
GREAT MEALS IN MINUTES
THE CIVIL WAR
PLANET EARTH
COLLECTOR'S LIBRARY OF THE CIVIL WAR
THE EPIC OF FLIGHT
THE GOOD COOK
WORLD WAR II
HOME REPAIR AND IMPROVEMENT
THE OLD WEST

This volume is one of a series that examines
various aspects of computer technology
and the role computers play in modern life.

COVER

Bearing an array of numbers, symbols and
seemingly cryptic commands, the keys of a
modern personal computer stand ready to
transmit instructions to the machine's
central processing unit.

UNDERSTANDING COMPUTERS

Computer Basics

BY THE EDITORS OF TIME-LIFE BOOKS

TIME-LIFE BOOKS, ALEXANDRIA, VIRGINIA

Contents

Building Up to the Computer Revolution

Human beings have always needed to count. In the dim millennia of prehistory, people had to make do with counting on their fingers or scratching marks on bone. By about 4,000 years ago, early civilizations had developed sophisticated numbering systems to keep track of commercial transactions, astronomical cycles and other matters. Manual calculating tools appeared a few millennia later. And today, computations of prodigious complexity — as well as a whole host of jobs apparently unrelated to numbers — are performed by the sophisticated "electronic brains" called computers.

Experts are quick to point out that a computer is not really a brain (or at least, some would add, not yet). Rather, it is simply another tool, another piece of machinery devised to reduce labor or extend our mastery of the world. For all its seeming brilliance, a modern computer's sole talent is to react with lightning speed to coded bursts of voltage. The true brilliance is human: the genius of men and women who have found a way to translate a variety of information from the real world into the zeros and ones of the binary code — the logical and mathematical language tailor-made for a computer's electronic circuitry.

Still, no other machine in history has so rapidly or so thoroughly changed the world. Computers have made possible such epic achievements as lunar landings and planetary probes, and they account for myriad everyday conveniences and benefits. They monitor anesthesia in hospitals, help children learn to read in schools, create special effects for the movies. They have replaced or supplemented the typewriter in newsrooms and the adding machine in banks. They enhance television reception, control telephone networks and record the price of groceries at the supermarket check-out counter. In short, they are woven into the very fabric of modern life, making computer avoidance, if not computer ignorance, practically impossible.

Recent gains in computer power and versatility have come at a dizzying rate, spurred by the appearance in the early 1970s of a tiny technological miracle called the microprocessor. On this chip of silicon — smaller even than a baby's fingernail — reside hundreds of thousands of electronic components capable of outperforming the room-sized dinosaurs that had dominated the computer world only a few years before.

Despite the head-spinning pace of modern advances, the foundations of the computer revolution were built in slow and fitful fashion. A starting point was the development — more than 1,500 years ago, and probably in the Mediterranean world — of the abacus, an arrangement of beads and rods used by merchants for counting and calculating. In arithmetical terms, the rods of an abacus act as place columns: Each bead on the ones rod is worth one, those on the 10s rod are worth

Like a visual echo of the computer's growing role in modern society, multi-colored outlines radiate from a silhouetted human figure in this Japanese example of the special effects available through computer graphics. The original profile was created by an illustrator, then manipulated by a designer using a computer process called vector graphics to simulate dynamic motion.

7

10 apiece, and so on. The abacus was so efficient that it soon spread far and wide, and in some lands it is still in use. Not until the 17th Century, a time of great intellectual ferment, did it meet significant competition as a computational tool.

European thinkers of that era were fascinated by the challenge of devising aids to calculation. Among the most resourceful was John Napier of Scotland, a theologian, mathematician and would-be designer of military weapons who once tried to design a sort of death ray: a system of mirrors and lenses arranged to produce a lethal beam of concentrated sunlight. Of more lasting import was the publication in 1614 of his discovery of logarithms. A logarithm is the exponent of a base number, indicating to what power that base must be raised to produce another given number. Napier realized that any number can be expressed in these terms. For example, 100 is 10^2, and 23 is $10^{1.36173}$. Furthermore, Napier found that the logarithm of a plus the logarithm of b equals the logarithm of a times b — a truth that transformed complex multiplication problems into simpler addition problems. Someone multiplying two large numbers need only look up their logarithms in a log table, add the logarithms together and find the number that corresponds to that sum in a reverse, or antilog, table.

Napier's tables — which themselves required tedious computation to create — were later combined into a handy device for rapid calculation: the slide rule, developed in the late 1620s by William Oughtred, among others. For his own part, Napier came up with a different (nonlogarithmic) aid to multiplication in 1617, the year he died. Known as Napier's bones, it consisted of a set of segmented rods that could be arranged so that the answer to a multiplication problem could be found by adding numbers in horizontally adjacent sections.

PASCAL'S WHEELS AND COGS

Although Napier's theory of logarithms would have enduring application, the bones were soon eclipsed by the slide rule and other types of calculators — most notably, a mechanical type pioneered by a brilliant Frenchman named Blaise Pascal. The son of a regional tax official, Pascal was only 19 when he began work on an adding machine in 1642; he was inspired in the attempt by the computational drudgery of his father's job. Before he died at the age of 39, he had earned a high place in history as a mathematician, physicist, writer and philosopher. One of today's computer programming languages is named in his honor.

Pascal's machine, the Pascaline, was a boxed wheel-and-cog device; he built more than 50 versions of it over the course of a decade. The operator fed it the figures to be added by dialing them on a series of wheels. Each wheel, marked with the digits zero through nine, stood for a particular decimal column — ones, 10s, 100s and so on. A wheel "carried" a total greater than nine by executing a complete turn and advancing the higher-order wheel to its left by one digit. It performed other operations by a cumbersome system of repetitive additions.

Though widely praised, the Pascaline did not make Pascal rich. Nevertheless, his principle of interlocking wheels remained central to the operation of most adding machines for the next 300 years.

The Pascaline's most serious drawback was its convoluted method of performing any calculations other than simple addition. The first machine that could do subtraction, multiplication and division easily was invented later in the century by a German genius whose imagination seemed to spawn no end of original

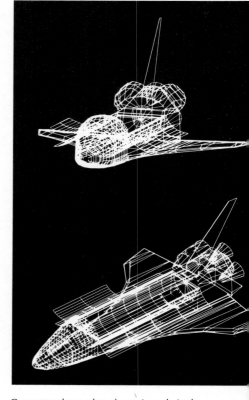

Computers have played a major role in the design, testing and operation of the space shuttle, shown here in computer-generated drawings. Visual models like these, projected in three dimensions, are also used by architects, medical researchers and engineers. The models can be manipulated on the screen to simulate stress tests on structural parts or to display molecular alterations for chemical research. Similarly, models integrated into realistic visual simulators help train pilots, gun crews and air-traffic controllers.

ideas. Gottfried Wilhelm Leibniz was born in 1646 in Leipzig to a family of scholars and government officials. His father, a professor of moral philosophy, died when the boy was only six, but by that time Leibniz was well embarked on his journey of learning. He spent his days reading through the books in his late father's library, mastering history, Latin, Greek and other subjects on his own.

When he entered the University of Leipzig at the age of 15, he already possessed erudition rivaling that of many of his professors. Yet new worlds opened up to him there. At the university, he stumbled for the first time on the works of Johannes Kepler, Galileo and other scholars who were rapidly advancing the frontiers of scientific knowledge. The pace of progress in science thrilled him, and he added mathematics to his curriculum.

At the ripe age of 20, Leibniz was offered a professorship at the University of Nuremberg. He turned down the academic life to embark instead on a career in international diplomacy. But as he rattled by coach from one European capital to another, his restless mind pondered questions in such varied fields as ethics, hydraulics and astronomy. In 1672, while spending some time in Paris, Leibniz began studying with the Dutch mathematician and astronomer Christian Huygens. The experience fueled a determination to find a mechanical way of alleviating an astronomer's endless computation chores. "For it is unworthy of excellent men," Leibniz wrote, "to lose hours like slaves in the labor of calculation which could safely be relegated to anyone else if machines were used."

He produced his mechanical calculator in 1673. It had three significant elements. The adding portion was essentially identical to the Pascaline, but Leibniz included a movable component (a forerunner of the movable carriage in later desk calculators) and a hand crank on the side that drove a stepped wheel — or, in later versions, cylinders — in the interior works. This mechanism functioned with the movable component to speed the repetitive additions involved in multiplying or dividing. The repetition itself became automatic.

Leibniz demonstrated his machine before the French Academy of Sciences and the Royal Society of London. A model found its way to Peter the Great of Russia, who in turn passed it along to the Emperor of China as a first-rate example of Western technology. As well received as his device was, Leibniz eventually became better known for such accomplishments as the invention of calculus (independently worked out by Isaac Newton in England) and the perfection of binary arithmetic — something others would eventually apply to mechanical calculating.

A SILK WEAVER'S LEGACY

The next great advance had nothing to do with numbers — initially, anyway. Throughout the 18th Century, French silk weavers had experimented with schemes for guiding their looms by perforated tape, punched cards or wooden drums. In all three systems, the presence or absence of holes created patterns in the fabric by controlling the way the yarns were raised or lowered. In 1804, Joseph Marie Jacquard built a fully automated loom that could handle enormously complicated designs. The loom was programmed by a mountain of punched cards, each card controlling a single throw of the shuttle. To produce a new pattern, the operator simply replaced one set of cards with another. The Jacquard loom revolutionized the weaving industry and, in its essential features, is still used today. But punched cards were destined to have their greatest impact in the programming of computers.

Of all the pre-20th Century thinkers and tinkerers who added something to the development of computing, the one who came closest to actually inventing a computer in the modern sense was an Englishman named Charles Babbage. Born into a wealthy Devonshire family in 1791, Babbage earned fame for both the keenness of his mind and the crankiness of his personality. For 13 years this eccentric genius occupied the same Cambridge chair of mathematics once held by Isaac Newton, yet in all that time he never lived at the university or delivered a single lecture there. He was a founding member of the Royal Astronomical Society, wrote on subjects ranging from politics to manufacturing techniques, and helped develop such practical devices as the tachometer and the railroad cowcatcher. Babbage brought his intellect to bear on the sober problems of mortality rates and postal reform — and also on less weighty problems. For years he waged a losing campaign against organ-grinders, whose noise he hated so intensely that when he died the London *Times* described him as a man who had survived to almost 80 "in spite of organ-grinding persecutions."

But the cause that ultimately governed Babbage's life was the pursuit of mathematical accuracy. He made something of a crusade out of spotting errors in the published log tables used as aids to calculation by astronomers, mathematicians and navigators. Nothing was safe from his zeal. He once wrote the poet Alfred Lord Tennyson to upbraid him for the lines, "Every moment dies a man / Every moment one is born." Since the population of the world was not holding constant, Babbage pointed out, the lines would better and more truthfully read, "Every moment dies a man / Every moment one and one-sixteenth is born."

It was Charles Babbage's great glory and lifelong frustration to have conceived the fundamental principles of the modern computer a century before the technology existed to build one. He spent many decades, much government money and a good deal of his private fortune in the attempt.

A GRAND PLAN AND CRUSHED HOPES

In 1822, Babbage built a preliminary model of a device he called the Difference Engine, a machine that could compute lengthy scientific tables by means of toothed wheels on shafts turned by a crank. The same year he enlisted the Royal Society—a prestigious association of scientists—in a bid for a government grant to construct a full-scale working version. The machine, he wrote the Society's president, would take on the "intolerable labor and fatiguing monotony" involved in repetitive mathematical chores; these, he added, rank among the "lowest occupations of the human intellect." The Society judged his work "highly deserving of public encouragement," and a year later the British government awarded him £1,500 for the project.

For the next 10 years Babbage wrestled with his brainchild. He originally expected to finish it in three years, but the Difference Engine grew increasingly complex as he modified, enhanced and redesigned it. Labor, health and money problems beset him. Though government grants eventually swelled to £17,000, official doubts about the project's expense and ultimate usefulness also grew. In the end, the grants were halted, although many years passed before the government formally told Babbage that there would be no more money for his machine.

The computer's most significant predecessors appear on the time line that begins at right and continues on the following two pages. Some of the eight devices shown aimed to make mathematical calculations and tabulations easier and faster. Others contributed methods that were eventually used for putting information into computing machines and for controlling more complex processes. Of all the devices, only the abacus, oldest of the eight, is still employed today, in parts of the Soviet Union, the Orient and the Middle East.

By 1833, Babbage was ready to put aside his plans for the Difference Engine. Considering its troubled history, that was hardly surprising. Yet he went on to develop ideas for an even more ambitious machine. The Analytical Engine, unlike its predecessor, was designed not just to solve one type of mathematical problem but to carry out a wide range of calculating tasks according to the instructions supplied by its operator. It was to be "a machine of the most general nature" — nothing less, in fact, than the first general-purpose programmable computer.

The Analytical Engine was to have a "mill" and a "store," both composed of cogs and wheels. The store would hold up to 100 forty-digit numbers at a time. Numbers would be kept in the store until their turn came to be operated on in the mill; results would then be moved back into the store to await further use or to be printed out. Instructions would be fed into the Analytical Engine by means of punched cards. "We may say most aptly that the Analytical Engine weaves *algebraical patterns* just as the Jacquard-loom weaves flowers and leaves," wrote the Countess of Lovelace, one of the few people who comprehended both the machine's methods and its vast potential for application.

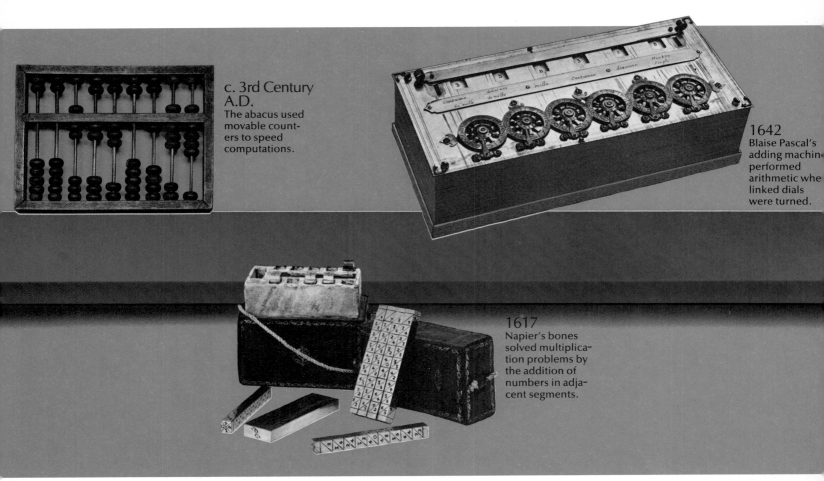

c. 3rd Century A.D.
The abacus used movable counters to speed computations.

1642
Blaise Pascal's adding machine performed arithmetic when linked dials were turned.

1617
Napier's bones solved multiplication problems by the addition of numbers in adjacent segments.

Born Augusta Ada Byron, the only legitimate child of the poet Lord Byron, the Countess of Lovelace lent her considerable talents for mathematics and writing to Babbage's project. Regarding the Analytical Engine, Babbage declared that Lovelace "seems to understand it better than I do, and is far, far better at explaining it." What she understood best was the machine's radical conception — that it was indeed a mathematical Jacquard loom: essentially empty, but capable of executing any pattern or program that could be translated onto punched cards.

The Countess of Lovelace helped Babbage to clarify his ideas and lifted his spirits by her interest and enthusiasm. But even she could not write or charm away the Analytical Engine's fundamental problem. If the Difference Engine had been a doubtful proposition, the Analytical Engine was an impossibility. Parts simply could not be made to run it. The finished machine would have been as big as a locomotive, its insides an intricate mass of intermeshing steel, brass and pewter clockwork, all driven by steam. The least imbalance in the smallest part would have been multiplied hundreds of times over, dooming the machine to violent seizure.

The Analytical Engine was never built. All that exists of it are reams of plans and

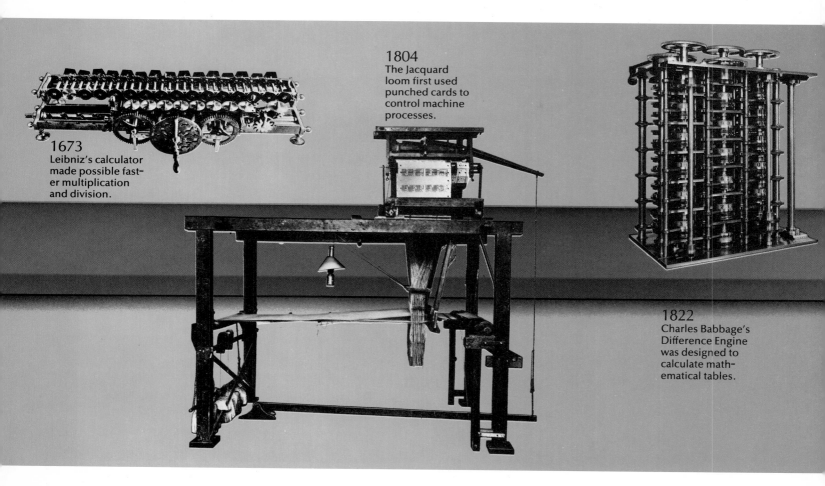

1804
The Jacquard loom first used punched cards to control machine processes.

1673
Leibniz's calculator made possible faster multiplication and division.

1822
Charles Babbage's Difference Engine was designed to calculate mathematical tables.

drawings and a small portion of the mill and printer built by Babbage's son.

Ironically, the Difference Engine fared somewhat better. Though Babbage himself never returned to it, a Swedish printer, inventor and translator named Georg Scheutz read of the device and built a modified version of it with Babbage's generous advice. In what was doubtless a bittersweet experience, Babbage finally saw his—or their—creation perform in London in 1854. A year later, the Scheutz Difference Engine won a gold medal at the Exhibition of Paris; a few years after that, the British government that had backed and abandoned Babbage commissioned one for its Registrar-General's Department.

Just 19 years after Babbage's death, one aspect of the Analytical Engine — punched cards — appeared in a functioning machine. The machine was a statistical tabulator built by the American Herman Hollerith to speed up the processing of returns for the 1890 U.S. census. The son of German immigrants, Hollerith was born in Buffalo, New York. In 1879 he finished his studies at Columbia University's School of Mines and went to work for the census office in Washington. He arrived just in time to watch hundreds of clerks begin what would be a laborious seven and a half year struggle to tabulate the 1880 census by hand.

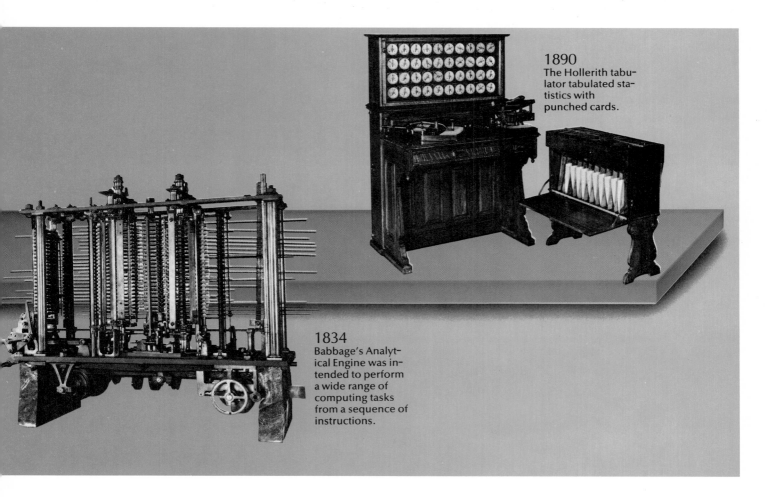

1890
The Hollerith tabulator tabulated statistics with punched cards.

1834
Babbage's Analytical Engine was intended to perform a wide range of computing tasks from a sequence of instructions.

John Shaw Billings, a high-ranking census official and Hollerith's future father-in-law, suggested that the tabulation might be done with punched cards, and Hollerith spent the 1880s working to develop such a system. It is not known where Billings himself got the idea — from Jacquard's loom, perhaps, or from watching railroad conductors punch tickets — but he was content to let Hollerith pursue it. By 1890, Hollerith had perfected his system: In a census office speed contest, his statistical tabulator bested several rivals to win the 1890 census contract and forge a new link in the chain of computer history.

The cards in Hollerith's tabulator were the size of dollar bills. Each card had 12 rows of 20 holes to be punched for the data on age, sex, country of birth, number of children, occupation, marital status and everything else the census wanted to know about the U.S. population. Canvassers in the field carried forms on which to record the answers to these questions. The forms were sent to Washington, where the information was transferred to the cards by punching the appropriate holes. Fed into another device hooked up to the tabulating machines, the punched cards were pressed onto ranks of fine pins, one for each of the 240 items on a card; when a pin found a hole, it pushed through to dip into a small cup of mercury, thereby completing an electrical circuit and causing an indicator on a bank of recording dials to move forward one place.

SPRINGBOARD TO SUCCESS

So swift was Hollerith's machine that a simple count was ready in six weeks, and a full statistical analysis in two and a half years. The population had grown by nearly 13 million people over the previous decade, to a total of 62,622,250; yet the 1890 census took roughly a third as long as its predecessor to tabulate.

Hollerith won prizes, praise and a doctorate from Columbia for his invention. "The apparatus," marveled the *Electrical Engineer,* "works as unerringly as the mills of the Gods, but beats them hollow as to speed." Hollerith himself boasted of being "the first statistical engineer," as indeed he was. He formed the Tabulating Machine Company to lease his invention to railroads, government offices and even tsarist Russia, which had decided that it, too, wanted a modern census.

The company was immediately and lastingly successful; over the years, it passed through a number of mergers and name changes. The last came in 1924, five years before Herman Hollerith died, and created the International Business Machines Corporation, or IBM. Now, a century and a half after Charles Babbage's epic struggle with the Analytical Engine, IBM is a world leader in an industry that has brought to life his vision of "a machine of the most general nature." Even Babbage's fertile mind could not have foreseen the forms his dream machine would ultimately take.

New Genies for the Age of Automation

Through the 20th Century magic of miniaturization, more and more everyday objects and tools possess a kind of resident genie, a phenomenally small computing device called a microprocessor. Popularly known as a microchip, a microprocessor is a far cry from clumsy ancestors like Pascal's adding machine or the Hollerith tabulator. The modern device is an electronic powerhouse composed of hundreds of thousands of microscopic electrical circuits etched on a tiny sliver of silicon.

Semiconductor companies sometimes spend millions of dollars developing a microprocessor design, but mass production may allow the chip to be sold for a few dollars. Other manufacturers then build the little wizards into an enormous variety of products, a few of which can be seen on the following pages.

A microprocessor works by responding to electrical impulses that open and close its circuits thousands or millions of times per second. Each opening or closing represents a single unit of information, encoded in the digits zero or one of the binary number system *(Chapter 2)*. The chip is thus a "digital" device, only interpreting information that is presented as individual bits, or binary digits, rather than perceiving it as a smooth, or "analog," continuum. Like the dots and dashes of Morse code, the opened and closed circuits of a microprocessor can combine to spell out instructions for machines as diverse as automatic coffee makers and personal computers. So ubiquitous has the tiny digital genie become that millions of times a day, people take part in the computer revolution by acts as mundane as making a telephone call, starting their cars, passing through a supermarket check-out counter, or merely checking the time on a wrist watch.

The Secrets of a Digital Watch

Scientists tending their gargantuan machines at the dawn of the modern computer age could hardly have imagined a day when people would casually strap $10 computers around their wrists. But the miracle of the microchip has made that unlikely day possible, transforming the once-fallible wrist watch into a device that not only is extraordinarily accurate but also can take on all sorts of new roles.

Traditional watches use balance wheels, springs and gears to keep time. Electronic watches have replaced those innards with a microprocessor, a quartz crystal and a battery. Thanks to these new parts, computerized watches never have to be wound, and they should be accurate to within three minutes a year (a traditional watch may lose three minutes a week).

In a computer-controlled watch, the microchip counts off the seconds and sends signals to the watch face, which may be either a traditional analog face or a new-style digital one. In the analog type, the signals move mechanical hands around the face to represent time as a continuous function. In the digital type, time appears numerically — 12:01:03, 12:01:04, 12:01:05 — as the microchip signals electrodes that charge a liquid crystal display *(opposite)*. This task alone requires the chip to process more than 30,000 pieces of information per second. Astoundingly, that represents only a fraction of the chip's power. More than enough remains to enable the watch to perform as a calendar, stop watch or alarm clock. Some watches can instantaneously switch from telling time to serving as calculators or video games. And a microprocessor may also become a sort of electronic diary, offering storage space, or "memory," for notes on important telephone numbers, appointments, birthdays and any other crucial information the busy wearer cannot afford to forget.

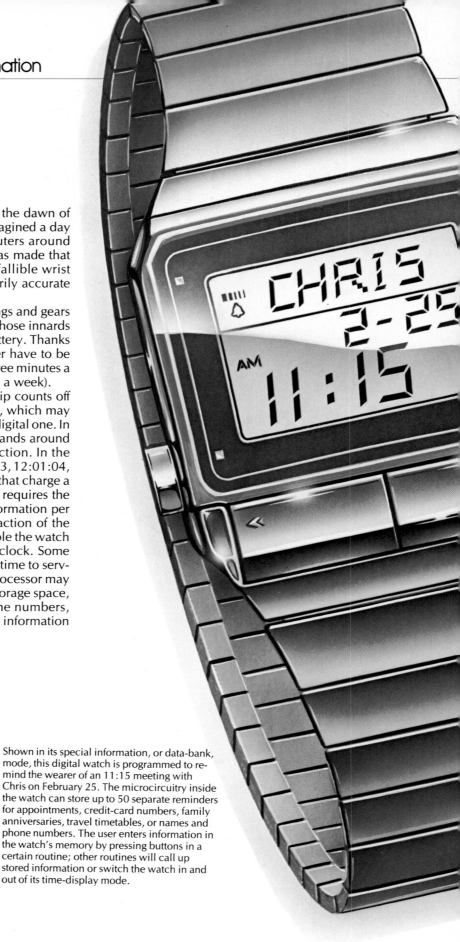

Shown in its special information, or data-bank, mode, this digital watch is programmed to remind the wearer of an 11:15 meeting with Chris on February 25. The microcircuitry inside the watch can store up to 50 separate reminders for appointments, credit-card numbers, family anniversaries, travel timetables, or names and phone numbers. The user enters information in the watch's memory by pressing buttons in a certain routine; other routines will call up stored information or switch the watch in and out of its time-display mode.

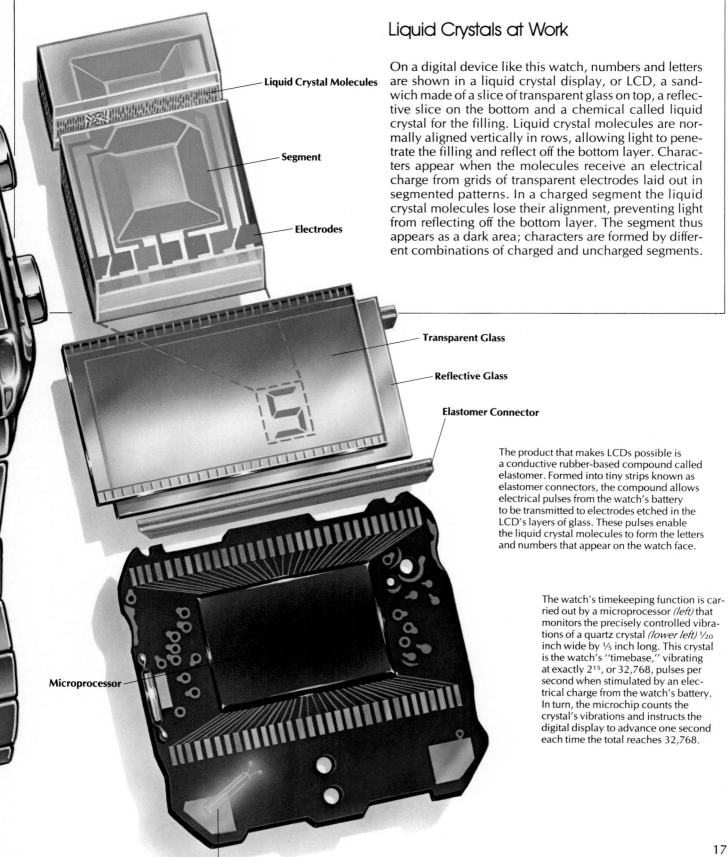

Liquid Crystals at Work

On a digital device like this watch, numbers and letters are shown in a liquid crystal display, or LCD, a sandwich made of a slice of transparent glass on top, a reflective slice on the bottom and a chemical called liquid crystal for the filling. Liquid crystal molecules are normally aligned vertically in rows, allowing light to penetrate the filling and reflect off the bottom layer. Characters appear when the molecules receive an electrical charge from grids of transparent electrodes laid out in segmented patterns. In a charged segment the liquid crystal molecules lose their alignment, preventing light from reflecting off the bottom layer. The segment thus appears as a dark area; characters are formed by different combinations of charged and uncharged segments.

Liquid Crystal Molecules

Segment

Electrodes

Transparent Glass

Reflective Glass

Elastomer Connector

The product that makes LCDs possible is a conductive rubber-based compound called elastomer. Formed into tiny strips known as elastomer connectors, the compound allows electrical pulses from the watch's battery to be transmitted to electrodes etched in the LCD's layers of glass. These pulses enable the liquid crystal molecules to form the letters and numbers that appear on the watch face.

Microprocessor

The watch's timekeeping function is carried out by a microprocessor *(left)* that monitors the precisely controlled vibrations of a quartz crystal *(lower left)* $1/20$ inch wide by $1/3$ inch long. This crystal is the watch's "timebase," vibrating at exactly 2^{15}, or 32,768, pulses per second when stimulated by an electrical charge from the watch's battery. In turn, the microchip counts the crystal's vibrations and instructs the digital display to advance one second each time the total reaches 32,768.

Quartz Crystal

A Camera with Electronic Reflexes

Automatic cameras have been around since the 1930s, when the introduction of selenium cells — light-sensitive electronic devices — made built-in light meters possible. Later, the advent of transistors brought automated shutter control; with further miniaturization, electronic elements — and the cameras that house them — have grown ever more sophisticated. Nowadays, a computerized camera can do almost everything for the photographer except urge the subject to smile.

A computerized camera like the one illustrated here frees the photographer from worries about overexposed or underexposed images, relieving the amateur's anxiety and allowing the professional to respond with split-second timing to shifting action or light. As fast as the photographer can focus the lens and press the shutter release, the camera can calculate light readings and select the ideal aperture and exposure setting from tens of thousands of options.

The key to the camera's reflexes is a sophisticated microprocessor that controls other specialized chips and can juggle a huge number of variables in the blink of an eye. Unlike earlier automatic cameras, which took one light-intensity reading for each exposure and averaged it over the entire picture, this camera takes a light reading from five distinct segments for every picture and finds the optimum settings for that particular combination of five numbers. No longer is it possible for a bright object such as the sun in one corner of the frame to skew the entire calculation, resulting in an underexposed shot. As it analyzes the multiple readings, the microprocessor eliminates extremes at either end of the scale and chooses settings accordingly. Even tricky or unusual lighting situations can thus yield pictures that are properly exposed. The chip does not have the last word, however. A manual setting can override the camera's automatic responses and put the choice of shutter speed and aperture — and artistic effect — back in the photographer's control.

The photographs below illustrate the way the camera chooses settings for lens aperture and shutter speed. For the picture on the left, the camera was purposely set to take only one light reading, resulting in an image with extremely dark patches. For the more evenly exposed image on the right, light sensor cells *(opposite)* divided the subject into five sectors and took a separate reading from each one. The five brightness levels were translated into digital code, and the main microprocessor selected the right settings by comparing the readings with stored information extrapolated from the analysis of tens of thousands of photographs.

The decoder driver is the electronic translator that allows the camera to communicate with the photographer. When the camera's microcomputer has done its calculations, this device receives the coded results and changes them into signals that activate the liquid crystal display, or LCD, where the photographer can read the data.

A tiny liquid crystal display keeps the photographer apprised of the best available speed and aperture settings in each lighting situation. The LCD also flashes overexposure and underexposure warnings.

About the size of a thumbnail, this microprocessor is the brain of the computerized camera. The chip's high-speed calculations control shutter speed and aperture when the camera is operating in the automatic-exposure mode. When the photographer has opted for the manual setting, the microprocessor continues to generate the readings that appear on the LCD. It also controls five other microchips with specialized functions.

Light Sensor Cell

Light Sensor Cell

The variable resistor block contains devices used by the manufacturer to fine-tune the analog parts of the camera, such as the light metering system, shutter speed and flash.

When the camera is set on automatic, this chip is controlled by the main microprocessor to gather information on lens settings and exposure times. In manual mode, the chip works independently to help set shutter speed and exposure times.

Chips for Health and Fitness

Just as the chip has expanded the kinds of information obtainable from a wrist watch, it has also taken much of the bother out of performing some of the routine tests and measurements once confined to clinics, health clubs or diet centers. Health-conscious retirees can take their own blood pressure daily; fitness enthusiasts can monitor their heart rate; and anxious parents can check a feverish child's temperature without having to shake down a balky mercury thermometer.

Exercise equipment may now include microprocessors that do everything but tie your shoelaces. Given your pulse,

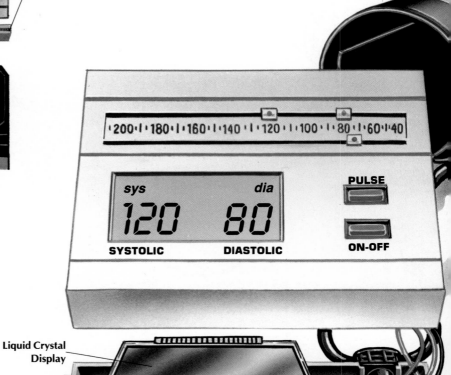

Liquid Crystal Display

Elastomer Connector's

98.6 °F

Microprocessor

Beeper

Cuff

PULSE

ON-OFF

sys 120 **dia** 80
SYSTOLIC **DIASTOLIC**

Liquid Crystal Display

Unlike a traditional thermometer, which represents body temperature by the height of a mercury column in a calibrated tube, a digital thermometer built around a microprocessor simply indicates the temperature as a numerical display. The thermometer's sensor perceives temperature as a continuous function; the microprocessor then converts the reading into digital terms and advances the easy-to-read LCD $^2/_{10}$ of a degree at a time. When the temperature has remained constant for a predetermined length of time, the reading is locked in and a beeper sounds.

Temperature Sensor

The pressure sensor in this computerized blood pressure meter registers heartbeats and the level of pressure exerted by the blood as it pumps against the air pressure in the inflatable cuff. Pulse rate as well as systolic and diastolic readings — measurements of blood pressure taken when the heart contracts and when it relaxes — are displayed on the meter's LCD when the measurement cycle is ended. Although the microprocessor is capable of checking and reporting blood pressure, it cannot replace a qualified medical interpretation of the reading.

Microprocessor **Pressure Sens**

age and weight, some indoor bicycles can estimate your oxygen uptake or calorie expenditure during exercise and show a constantly updated reading on a convenient display. If dieting is part of the fitness regimen, you can weigh your mealtime portions on a sophisticated kitchen scale whose computer memory is packed with data on nutritional value and calorie content. Or you can monitor your weight on a computerized scale, entering your weight-loss goals and receiving feedback on your progress — or lack of it. Built-in instructions also enable the scale to forecast how many days it will take you to shed the desired poundage. Computerized home medical equipment such as digital thermometers and blood pressure gauges can help you perform your own routine health checks. Responsible equipment manufacturers are quick to point out, however, that these handy tools do not replace professional care. If self-examination reveals anything amiss, you are urged to visit a doctor's office — where you are likely to encounter an array of computerized equipment even more sophisticated than what you might have at home.

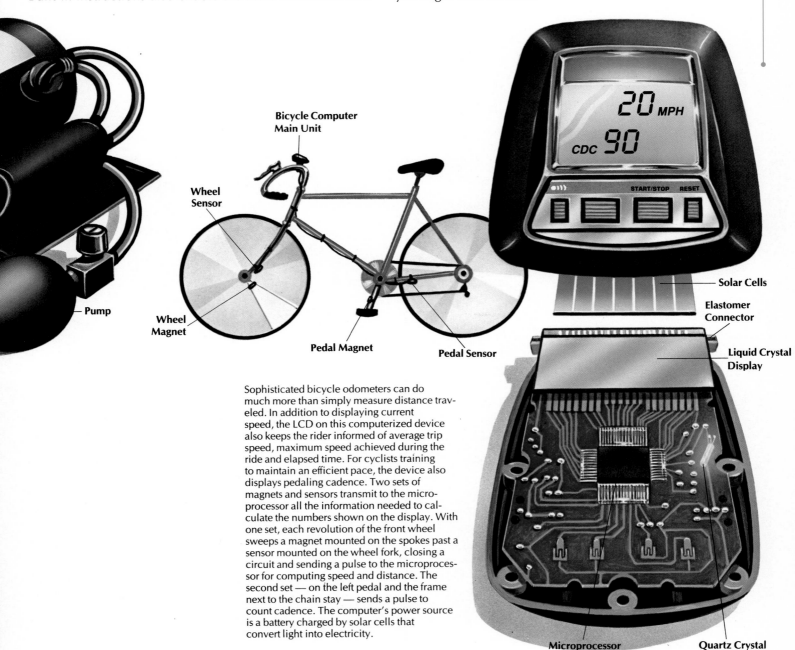

Pump

Bicycle Computer Main Unit

Wheel Sensor

Wheel Magnet

Pedal Magnet

Pedal Sensor

20 MPH

CDC 90

START/STOP   RESET

Solar Cells

Elastomer Connector

Liquid Crystal Display

Microprocessor

Quartz Crystal

Sophisticated bicycle odometers can do much more than simply measure distance traveled. In addition to displaying current speed, the LCD on this computerized device also keeps the rider informed of average trip speed, maximum speed achieved during the ride and elapsed time. For cyclists training to maintain an efficient pace, the device also displays pedaling cadence. Two sets of magnets and sensors transmit to the microprocessor all the information needed to calculate the numbers shown on the display. With one set, each revolution of the front wheel sweeps a magnet mounted on the spokes past a sensor mounted on the wheel fork, closing a circuit and sending a pulse to the microprocessor for computing speed and distance. The second set — on the left pedal and the frame next to the chain stay — sends a pulse to count cadence. The computer's power source is a battery charged by solar cells that convert light into electricity.

A Car's Computerized Nerve System

Located under the dashboard, this computer is one of two major computer systems in the car. Along with two specialized subunits, it monitors more than a dozen functions *(green lines)*. One subunit keeps the car's interior temperature constant to within one degree and turns off the air-conditioning compressor when the engine needs extra power. The other subunit controls a digital fuel gauge that shows the average and current mile-per-gallon figures as well as the current tank level. The subunit also transmits information that enables the main computer to estimate the driving range, given the fuel level and speed.

This microprocessor directs the car's engine-control system *(yellow lines)*. Several thousand times each second, the computer checks such items as engine speed and battery voltage, and adjusts the precise air-to-fuel mixture reaching the cylinders. It also exchanges information with the car's other major computer system and switches on dashboard lights that warn the driver of malfunctions.

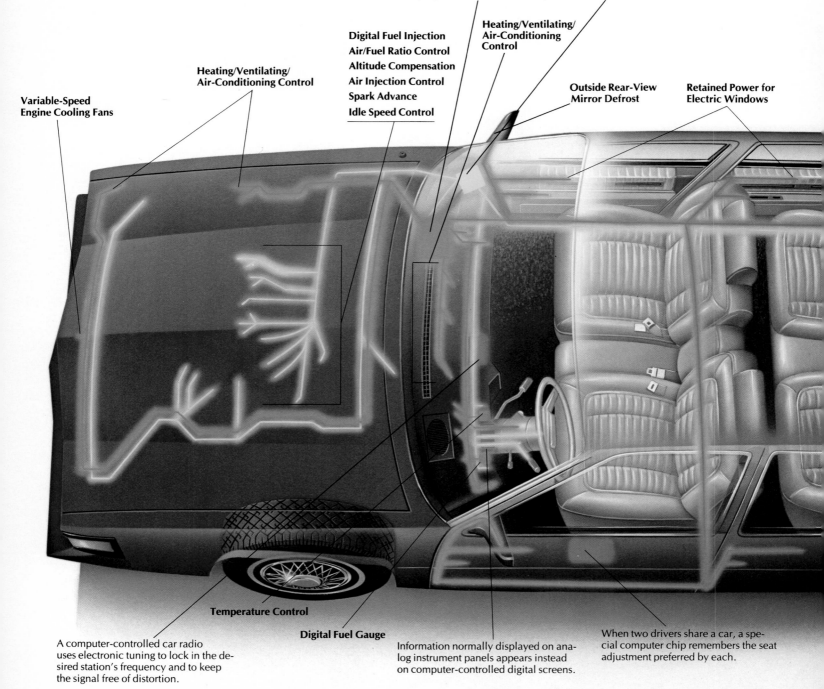

**Variable-Speed
Engine Cooling Fans**

**Heating/Ventilating/
Air-Conditioning Control**

**Digital Fuel Injection
Air/Fuel Ratio Control
Altitude Compensation
Air Injection Control
Spark Advance
Idle Speed Control**

**Heating/Ventilating/
Air-Conditioning
Control**

**Outside Rear-View
Mirror Defrost**

**Retained Power for
Electric Windows**

Temperature Control

Digital Fuel Gauge

A computer-controlled car radio uses electronic tuning to lock in the desired station's frequency and to keep the signal free of distortion.

Information normally displayed on analog instrument panels appears instead on computer-controlled digital screens.

When two drivers share a car, a special computer chip remembers the seat adjustment preferred by each.

The computerization of the automobile accelerated in the 1970s partly as a result of rising petroleum prices and concern about environmental pollution. With the advent of stricter standards for fuel efficiency and clean exhaust emissions, auto makers turned to microprocessors for help. By the mid-1980s, automotive assembly lines were producing cars fitted out with up to eight computers as standard equipment.

In the model shown here, a number of independent computer chips perform convenience functions such as adjusting the seats or fine-tuning the radio. Two sophisticated computers, capable of handling thousands of pieces of information a second, are employed to monitor and control the car's more essential systems. Sensors placed throughout the car's body and electrical system send signals back along special circuits to keep the computers informed of engine speed and temperature, the level of oxygen in the exhaust fumes and a host of other operating conditions — including potentially dangerous ones. In certain models, for example, sensors in the braking system can detect wheel lock in time to prevent the automobile from skidding out of control.

By monitoring components such as the starter, tachometer, odometer and coolant temperature gauge, a car's computers can in effect analyze a motorist's driving style and road habits: Does the driver tend to accelerate rapidly or gradually? How much of the driving consists of highway cruising and how much is stop-and-start in-town driving? The computer chip uses this battery of information to signal when certain systems or parts should be serviced. And when a computerized car goes to the garage for a tune-up or other maintenance, microchips that record significant averages or unusual events can present the mechanic with a complete diagnosis of the vehicle's service needs.

Intake Fuel Pump

Fuel-Level Sensor

Rear-Window Defrost

Retained Power for Trunk Release

Satellite Navigation

In the 21st Century, cars will navigate with the help of electronic links to satellites orbiting more than 12,500 miles above the earth. Each car's built-in antenna will receive satellite signals that an on-board computer will analyze to establish the vehicle's latitude, longitude and altitude above sea level. The computer will then retrieve one of several thousand maps from a storage disk and display the map on a screen. A symbol indicating the car's position will move as the car moves, and the computer will call up the next map as needed.

Unobtrusive Sentries for the Home

Computers designed to stand guard over a house range from devices that cost little more than $100 and that homeowners can install themselves, to systems that sell for several thousand dollars and require professional installation. The more expensive systems include the services of a central office that relays signals from the security computer to police or fire departments or to medical personnel.

The most sophisticated systems, like the one shown here, use smoke and heat sensors for fire protection, allow emergency calls to be sent at the touch of a button and set up a double defense against intruders. The first line of defense is located at the windows and doors. Here several methods can be used to detect unlawful entry, including magnetic sensors embedded in door or window frames, and shock sensors that pick up telltale vibrations such as those of shattering glass. A burglar who gets past these electronic watchdogs will still have to contend with pressure-sensitive floor mats, infrared detectors that pick up body heat from 40 feet away and ultrasonic installations that sense movement. The entire system runs on the normal electrical current of the house but has a backup battery to keep the premises protected if the power goes out.

The work of all the system's guardian gadgets is coordinated by a central computer unit programmed to respond to a variety of situations. If an influx of carbon particles or a rapid rise in temperature triggers smoke or heat sensors, the computer will transmit a signal for help over telephone lines and at the same time set off an alarm to alert anyone at home. If someone comes in through a protected door, the computer will wait a few seconds to see if the intruder is actually the homeowner, who knows a special identifying code to type in at one of the system's wall-mounted key pads. If the code is not forthcoming, the computer will send out its call for help. It will also let any intruders know that they have been discovered, sounding a piercing alarm or flashing the house lights on and off. If homeowners themselves detect an intruder, they can sound the alarm with conveniently located "panic buttons." And if they plan to be away for several days, they can program their security system to switch lights on and off at intervals that vary from day to day, giving the house an authentic lived-in look.

The control center of the security system is the main microprocessor, which monitors signals from all the sensing devices in the house. When alerted by a smoke, heat or intrusion sensor, it sets off the appropriate alarms within the house and also transmits a coded signal to a distant receiving station, where security workers can deal with the emergency. The home system's central computer also monitors the entire system for readiness and reports to the homeowner and to the receiving station if any device is malfunctioning.

Motion Detector

Alarm

This secondary command unit allows the homeowner to switch the system on and off and to monitor data from the central computer. The unit's microprocessor translates information about the rest of the house into flashing messages — such as warnings about a power failure, an open door or window, or a faulty circuit.

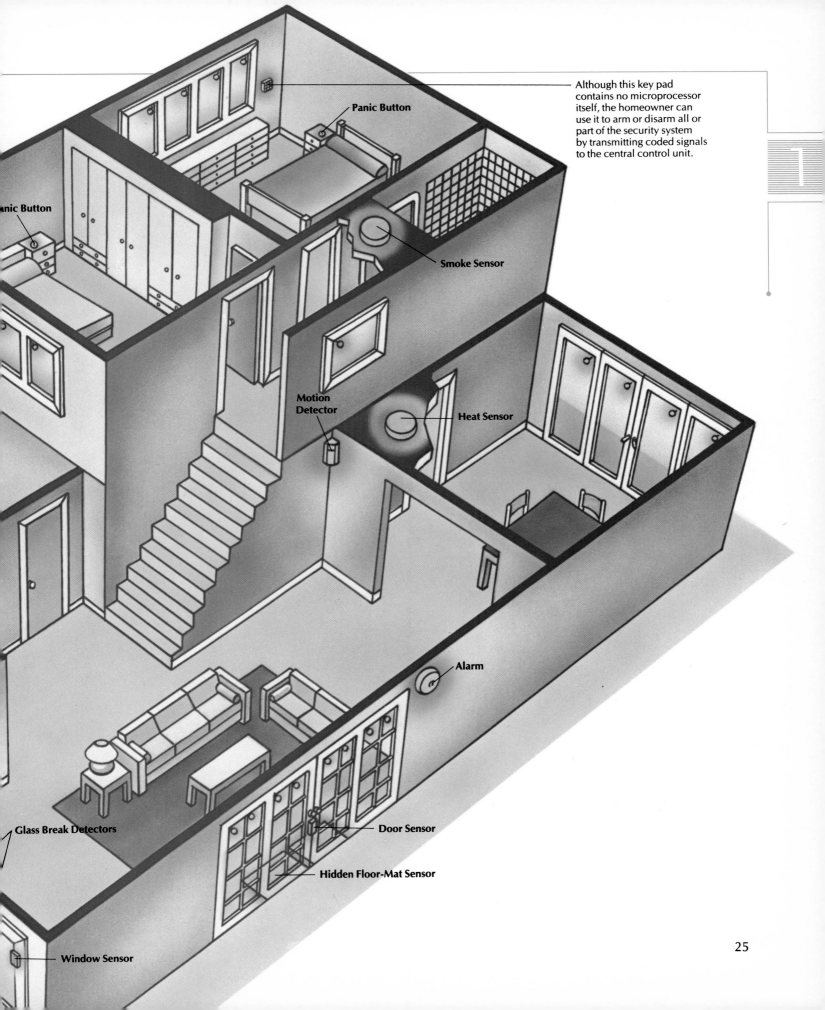

Panic Button

Panic Button

Although this key pad contains no microprocessor itself, the homeowner can use it to arm or disarm all or part of the security system by transmitting coded signals to the central control unit.

Smoke Sensor

Motion Detector

Heat Sensor

Alarm

Glass Break Detectors

Door Sensor

Hidden Floor-Mat Sensor

Window Sensor

A Desktop Generalist

The microchips inside cameras, cars, watches and the like are specialists, each programmed to carry out a limited set of tasks. The personal computer, on the other hand, is a generalist. Some of its chips are like those in a camera, with built-in instructions for running certain parts of the machine. But the chip that makes the personal computer such a powerful tool is a versatile microprocessor that shapes its work according to instructions received from the user. This central processing unit, as it is called, enables the computer to switch easily from playing an exciting video game to rearranging the paragraphs in a business report. Each role is defined and controlled by a set of electronically coded instructions called a program, or software.

Some computer users enjoy the challenge of writing their own programs, but most are content to choose from the thousands of software packages available on the market. With the help of different programs, personal computer users can track the performance of investment portfolios, organize tax records, store Christmas card lists or drill themselves in French verbs. They can bank, shop or run businesses from home. They can learn skills ranging from chess or bridge strategy to touch typing. By placing telephone calls to "data bases" maintained by other computers, personal computer users can do various kinds of research, riffling through distant electronic index files without leaving home or office. The personal computer, in short, is a servant of innumerable talents — not the least of them being that it is simple enough to be used by a six-year-old.

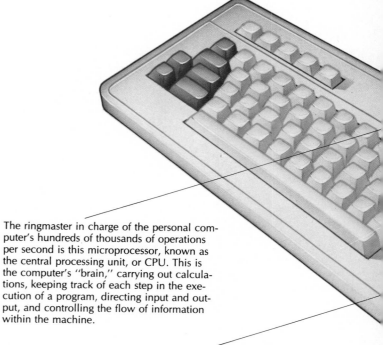

The ringmaster in charge of the personal computer's hundreds of thousands of operations per second is this microprocessor, known as the central processing unit, or CPU. This is the computer's "brain," carrying out calculations, keeping track of each step in the execution of a program, directing input and output, and controlling the flow of information within the machine.

Users commonly enter, or input, instructions to the computer by means of a typewriter-like keyboard equipped with extra keys to govern special computing functions. Other input devices include controllers such as a "joystick" or a "mouse" and monitor screens that respond to the touch of a finger.

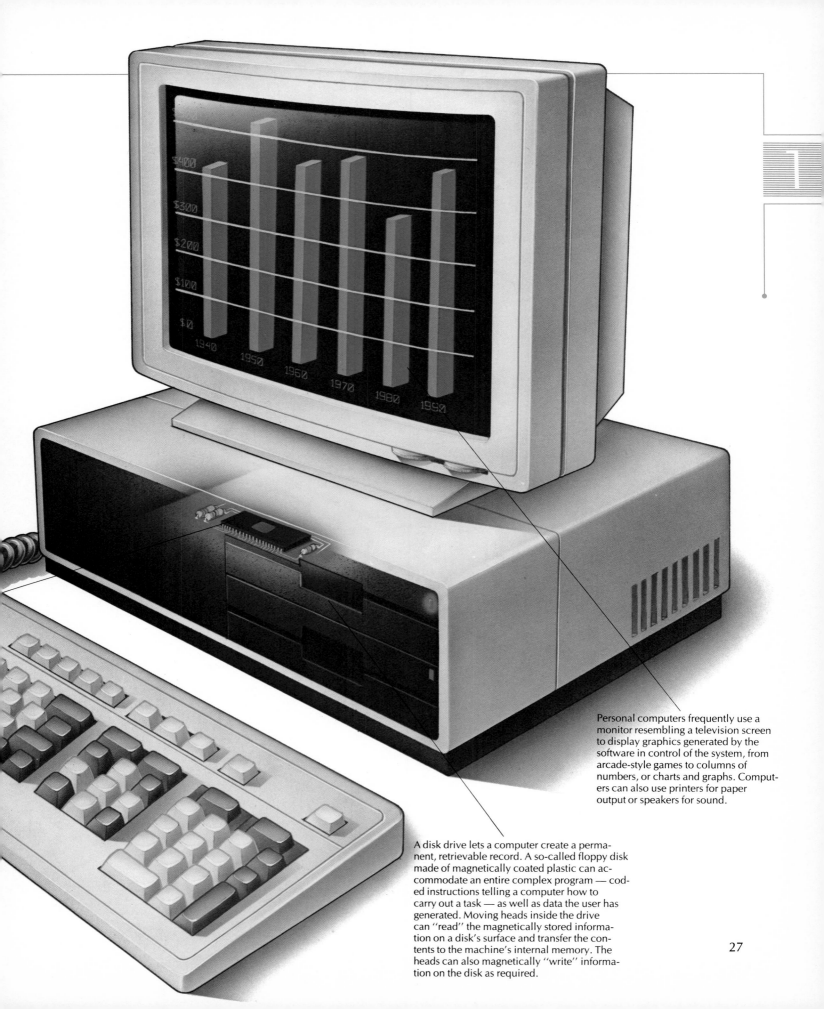

Personal computers frequently use a monitor resembling a television screen to display graphics generated by the software in control of the system, from arcade-style games to columns of numbers, or charts and graphs. Computers can also use printers for paper output or speakers for sound.

A disk drive lets a computer create a permanent, retrievable record. A so-called floppy disk made of magnetically coated plastic can accommodate an entire complex program — coded instructions telling a computer how to carry out a task — as well as data the user has generated. Moving heads inside the drive can "read" the magnetically stored information on a disk's surface and transfer the contents to the machine's internal memory. The heads can also magnetically "write" information on the disk as required.

27

```
00100010 01010100 01101000 01100001
00100111 01110011 00100000 01101111
01100101 00100000 01110011 01101101
01101100 01101100 00100000 01110011
01100101 01110000 00100000 01100110
01110010 00100000 01100001 00100000
01100001 01101110 00101100 00100000
01101110 01100101 00100000 01100111
01100001 01101110 01110100 00100000
01100101 01100001 01110000 00100000
01101111 01110010 00100000 01101101
01101110 01101011 01101001 01101110
00101110 00100010 00100000 00100000
01001110 01100101 01101001 01101100
01000001 01110010 01101101 01110011
01110010 01101111 01101110 01100111
00100000 01000001 01110000 01101111
01101100 01101111 00100000 00110001
```

0111 0100
0110 1110
0110 0001
0111 0100
0110 1111
0110 1101
0110 1111
0110 1001
0110 1100
0110 0110
0110 0001
0110 0100
0010 1101
0010 0000
0111 0100
0010 1100
0110 1100
0011 0001

The Power of the Binary Code

In July 1969, when the American astronaut Neil Armstrong realized the age-old human dream of reaching the moon, news of his achievement was instantaneously transmitted 240,000 miles across space to Houston, Texas, and then flashed to a waiting world. Television brought the scene into millions of living rooms, and news wires relayed the particulars—including Armstrong's brief and eloquent speech (left)—to thousands of newspapers and magazines around the globe. Much of the information traveled from machine to machine in a special code of on-off pulses, the electrical equivalents of zeros and ones.

Zeros and ones were a most appropriate link between the moon landing and earth's celebration of it, for the two symbols of the binary number system figured in that historic mission in thousands of ways, encoding everything from the commands that triggered takeoff to the instructions that kept Armstrong's spacecraft tilted at the proper angle for reentry into earth's atmosphere. And so it is in virtually every corner of our computer-dependent world. At root, any digital computer, no matter what its size or purpose, amounts to a trafficking system for information expressed in zeros and ones.

The idea of using just two symbols to encode information is an ancient one. The signal drums used by some African bush tribes sent messages via a combination of high and low pitches. The more recent Morse code, in which groups of dots and dashes represent the letters of the alphabet, is yet another two-symbol code. Australian aborigines counted by twos, and other hunter-gatherer groups from New Guinea to South America have handled arithmetic in the same way.

A two-symbol code is not the only alternative to a decimal system. Babylonian arithmetic was based on the number 60, and in the customs and language of English-speaking people are submerged the remnants of a 12-based system once dominant in the British Isles: 12 months in a year, 12 inches in a foot, two 12-hour periods in a day, measures of a dozen. Inspired by nothing more than the fingers on a pair of human hands, the decimal system eventually came to overshadow all other means of numeration, at least in the West. But certain Western thinkers of post-Renaissance times were fascinated by the two-state simplicity of binary

Encoded in zeros and ones, the first words spoken on the moon make sense only to a computer. Astronaut Neil Armstrong's statement — "That's one small step for a man, one giant leap for mankind" — is shown here translated into a code understood by most modern computers, the American Standard Code for Information Interchange, or ASCII (pages 32-35).

29

numbering. Slowly the concept filtered through separate scientific disciplines, from logic and philosophy to mathematics and then to engineering—to help usher in the dawn of the computer age.

One of the earliest champions of the binary system was the German genius Gottfried Wilhelm Leibniz, who came to it in a roundabout fashion. In 1666, while finishing his university studies and well before he invented his stepped-wheel calculator *(page 12)*, the 20-year-old Leibniz dashed off what he modestly described as a schoolboy's essay. Called "De Arte Combinatoria" ("On the Art of Combination"), this brief work laid out a general method for reducing all thinking—of any sort and on any subject—to statements of perfect exactitude. Logic (or, as he called it, the laws of thought) would be thus transposed from the verbal realm, which is loaded with ambiguities, to the dominion of mathematics, which can precisely define the relationships among objects or statements. In addition to proposing that all rational thinking be made mathematical, Leibniz called for "a sort of universal language or script, but infinitely different from all those projected hitherto; for the symbols and even the words in it would direct the reason; and errors, except those of fact, would be mere mistakes in calculation. It would be very difficult to form or invent this language or characteristic, but very easy to understand it without any dictionaries."

REFINING THE BINARY SYSTEM
His contemporaries, perhaps baffled, perhaps outraged by his notions, ignored the paper, and Leibniz himself apparently never pursued the idea of a new language. But a decade later, he began to explore the power of mathematics in a new way when he focused on refining the binary system. As he worked, laboriously transcribing row after row of numerals from decimal to binary, he was spurred by a centuries-old manuscript that had come to his attention. It was a commentary on the venerable Chinese *I Ching,* or *Book of Changes,* which seeks to portray the universe and all its complexities as a series of contrasting dualities—either / or propositions—among them dark and light, male and female. Encouraged by this apparent validation of his own mathematical notions, Leibniz proceeded to perfect and formalize the endless combinations of ones and zeros that make up the modern binary system.

For all his genius, however, Leibniz failed to find any immediate utility in the product of these labors. His stepped-wheel calculator had been designed to work with decimal numbers, and Leibniz never changed to binary numbers, perhaps daunted by the long strings of digits created by that system. Because only the digits zero and one are used, the decimal number eight, for instance, becomes 1000 when translated into binary, while the binary equivalent of the decimal 1,000 is an unwieldy 1111101000 *(pages 40-41).* Later Leibniz did give some thought to employing binary numbers in a computing device, but he never actually tried to build such a machine. Instead, he came to invest the binary system with mystical meaning, seeing in it the image of creation. To him, the number one represented God; zero stood for the void—the universe before anything other than God existed. From one and zero came everything, just as one and zero can express all mathematical ideas.

If it ever occurred to Leibniz that binary might be the all-purpose language of logic he had called for in his 1666 essay, he never said so. But a century and a

Early in the 19th Century, the self-taught British mathematician George Boole devised the system of symbolic logic called Boolean algebra. Nearly a century later, scientists would wed his formulas to the binary number system, making possible the electronic digital computer.

quarter after his death in 1716, a self-taught British mathematician named George Boole vigorously resumed the search for a universal language.

It is remarkable that a man of Boole's humble origins was able to take up such a quest. His parents were poor tradespeople in the industrial town of Lincoln in eastern England. In that time and place, a child of the working class had little hope of getting a solid education, much less of pursuing intellectual interests as a career. But Boole's determination was boundless.

There was a school for boys in Lincoln. Possibly Boole attended it; if so, he would have received only the most rudimentary sort of instruction. However, his father had taught himself a smattering of mathematics and was able to pass that knowledge along to his precocious son. By the age of eight, the lad was thoroughly addicted to learning. One subject that seemed essential to further advancement was Latin. In this, his parents could not help him, but a family friend who was a bookseller knew enough Latin grammar to get Boole started. When the bookseller had taught him all he knew, Boole went on by himself, and by the age of 12 he was translating Latin poetry. Within two more years he had conquered Greek; later he added French, German and Italian to his battery of languages.

In 1831, when he was 16 years old, Boole was forced to take a job to help out with the family finances. For four years he worked as a poorly paid assistant teacher, then made bold to open a school of his own. Finding that he had to learn more mathematics in order to stay ahead of his students, he began to study the mathematical journals in the library of a local scientific institute. There, Boole discovered that he had a natural gift for the subject. Poring through stacks of learned publications, he mastered the most abstruse mathematical ideas of his day. He also began to have some original ideas of his own. These he wrote up, all the while running his little school, and in 1839 a journal accepted one of his papers for publication. Over the next decade, Boole began to make a name for himself by producing a steady stream of articles. So highly regarded was his work that in 1849 the schoolmaster without a formal education was asked to join the mathematics faculty of Queen's College in Ireland.

INVESTIGATING THE LAWS OF THOUGHT

With more time now to think and write, Boole turned increasingly to the subject Leibniz had speculated on long before: placing logic under the sway of mathematics. Boole had already written an important paper on the concept, "The Mathematical Analysis of Logic," in 1847, and in 1854 he further refined his ideas in a work entitled "An Investigation of the Laws of Thought." His pathbreaking essays revolutionized the science of logic.

What Boole devised was a form of algebra, a system of symbols and rules applicable to anything from numbers and letters to objects or statements. With this system, Boole could encode propositions — statements that can be proved true or false — in symbolic language and then manipulate them in much the same way ordinary numbers can be manipulated.

The three most basic operations in Boolean algebra are called AND, OR and NOT (page 42). Although Boole's system includes many other operations — often called logic gates — these three are the only ones needed to add, subtract, multiply and divide, or to perform such actions as comparing symbols or numbers. The gates are binary in nature; they process just two kinds of entities — either truth or

A Standard for Communication

When you hit the letter *A* on a typewriter keyboard, a hammer strikes the ribbon and makes the letter appear in ink on the page. The process is strictly mechanical. Hitting the same key on a computer keyboard, however, generates a set of zeros and ones, which causes the letter to appear as a luminous display on the screen. Every part of the process after the initial tap of the key is electronic. Moreover, the zeros and ones used to encode the letter — or any other character or control function — are standardized. Computers can thus pass information back and forth without translation: They are using a shared electronic language.

In the United States, this shared language is called ASCII — the American Standard Code for Information Interchange. (Other countries use a slightly modified international version.) ASCII — it rhymes with "passkey" — assigns a string of seven zeros and ones (binary digits, or bits) to every upper- and lower-case letter of the alphabet, to the numerals of the decimal system and to an assortment of punctuation marks and control symbols. An eighth bit is either ignored or used as a check on the accuracy of transmission. (Here and in the coded quote on page 28 the eighth, or leftmost, bit has been set arbitrarily at zero.)

Seven significant bits provide 2^7, or 128, possible permutations of zeros and ones. The first 32 are reserved for such codes as "carriage return" and "backspace," used to control screen displays and printers. The remaining 96 are called the printable codes because all but the first and last — the ones for "space" and "delete" — produce visible characters.

ASCII is constructed so that certain bits signal one piece of information ("this is a capital letter" or "this is a numeric character"), while the rest specify which letter and which numeral. The ASCII code for the capital letter *A*, for example, is decimal 65, which translates into binary 01000001. Lower-case *a* in ASCII is decimal 97, or binary 01100001; the difference is in the three leftmost bits. On the old-fashioned blocks shown here and on the following pages, the ASCII code numbers that signal a specific alphanumeric character (A, B, C or 1, 2, 3, for example) have been highlighted.

B b
01000010 01100010

C c
01000011 01100011

E e
01000101 01100101

F f
01000110 01100110

G g
01000111 01100111

I i
01001001 01101001

J j
01001010 01101010

K k
01001011 01101011

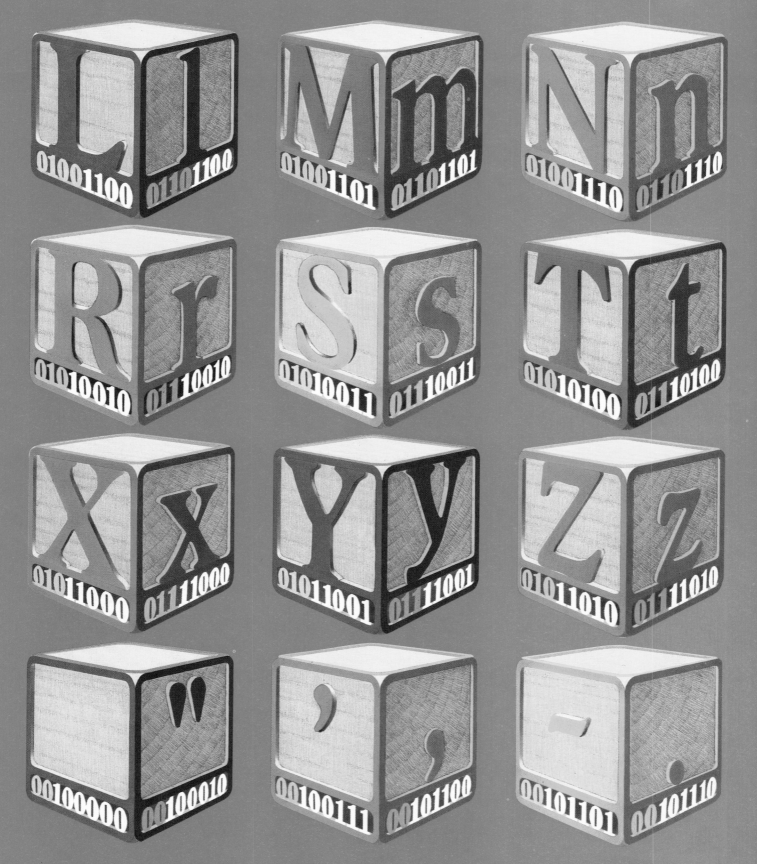

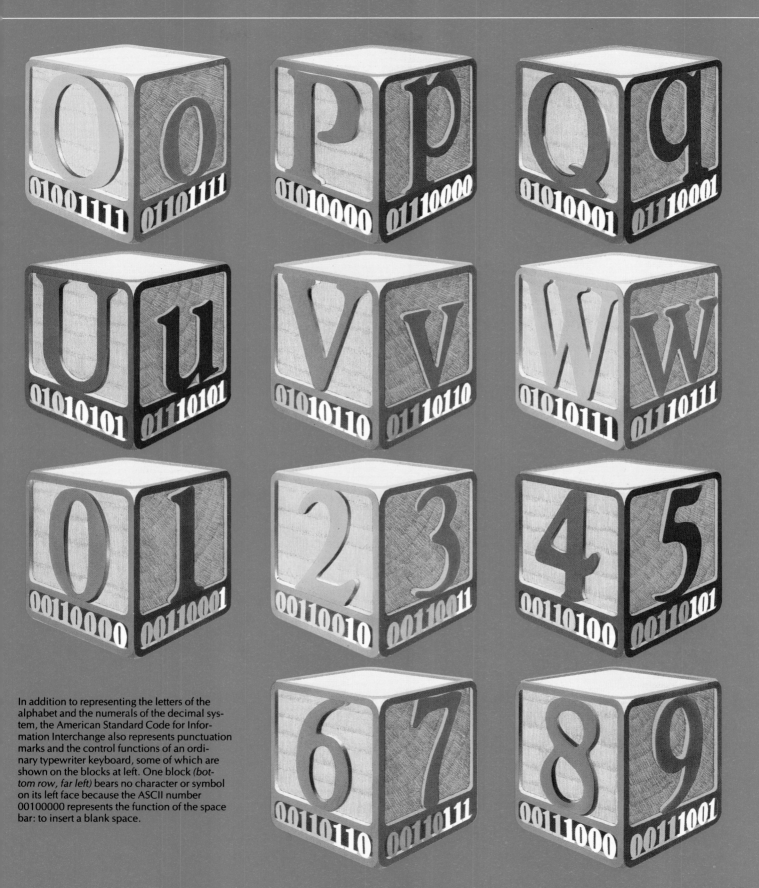

In addition to representing the letters of the alphabet and the numerals of the decimal system, the American Standard Code for Information Interchange also represents punctuation marks and the control functions of an ordinary typewriter keyboard, some of which are shown on the blocks at left. One block (bottom row, far left) bears no character or symbol on its left face because the ASCII number 00100000 represents the function of the space bar: to insert a blank space.

falsity, yes or no, open or closed, zero or one. Boole hoped that by stripping logical arguments of all verbiage, his system would make it far easier — practically a certainty, in fact — to arrive at a sound conclusion.

Most logicians of the time either ignored or criticized Boole's system, but it had a potency that could not long be resisted. An American logician named Charles Sanders Peirce introduced Boolean algebra to the United States in 1867, describing it briefly in a paper delivered to the American Academy of Arts and Sciences. Over the course of almost two decades, Peirce devoted much of his own time and energy to modifying and extending Boolean algebra. He realized that Boole's two-state logic lent itself easily to the description of electrical switching circuits: Currents were either on or off, just as a proposition was either true or false; a switch functioned much like a logic gate, either allowing current — i.e. truth — to proceed to the next switch or not. Peirce himself was ultimately more interested in logic than in the science of electricity. Although he later designed a rudimentary logic circuit using electricity, the device was never built.

TYING THEORY TO THE REAL WORLD
Still, by introducing Boolean algebra into American university courses in logic and philosophy, Peirce planted a seed that would bear fruit half a century later. In 1936, a 21-year-old American graduate student named Claude Shannon had an insight that bridged the gap between algebraic theory and practical application.

Shannon had only recently arrived at the Massachusetts Institute of Technology from the University of Michigan, where he had earned two bachelor's degrees, one in electrical engineering and the other in mathematics. To earn extra money at MIT, Shannon tended a cranky, cumbersome mechanical computing device known as a differential analyzer, built in 1930 by Shannon's professor, Vannevar Bush. The pioneering machine was the first to be able to solve complex differential equations — mathematical expressions for predicting the behavior of moving objects, such as airplanes, or of intangible forces, such as gravity. Such equations could take engineers months to work out by hand, and the differential analyzer was of great scientific importance. But it had major shortcomings. One was its size: Harking back to Babbage's Analytical Engine, Bush's analyzer was essentially a collection of shafts, gears and wires arranged in a succession of boxes that ran the length of a large room. But sheer size was not the analyzer's only drawback. The machine was also an analog device, meaning that it measured movement and distance, and performed its computations with these measurements. Setting up a problem required figuring out a multitude of gear ratios, which could take two or three days. Changing the problem was an equally tedious exercise of a day or more that required a screwdriver and a wrench and left a worker's hands covered in oil.

Bush had suggested that Shannon study the logical organization of the machine for his thesis, and as the student wrestled with the analyzer's balky innards, he could not help but consider ways to improve the device. Recalling the Boolean algebra he had studied as an undergraduate, Shannon was struck — as Peirce had been before him — by its similarity to the operation of an electric circuit. Shannon saw the implications for streamlining computer design. If electric circuits were laid out according to Boolean principles, they could then express logic and test the truth of propositions as well as carry out complex calculations.

Research by the mathematician Claude Shannon later inspired the binary code used by modern computers, in which the smallest unit of information is the bit—short for binary digit. Four bits are whimsically known as a nybble; two nybbles make up a byte, which many computers process as a single unit; some computer systems process larger groupings, or ''words.'' The byte here represents the decimal number 34. (In ASCII, it would represent quotation marks.)

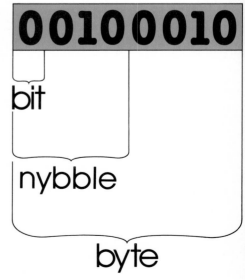

00100010

bit

nybble

byte

Electric circuits would certainly be an improvement over oily gears and shafts.

He pursued his ideas about binary numbers, Boolean algebra and electric circuitry in his master's thesis, which was published in 1938. This brilliant paper, which had an immediate effect on the design of telephone systems, ranks as a pivotal document in the development of modern computer science. (A decade later, Shannon published another seminal work — "A Mathematical Theory of Communication" — which described what has since come to be known as information theory. Shannon proposed a method of defining and measuring information in mathematical terms, as yes-no choices represented by binary digits — an idea that lies at the foundation of modern telecommunications.)

So great was the need for a workably proportioned machine that could solve difficult equations that three other researchers — two in the United States and one in Germany — were moving toward the same conclusions at almost the same moment. Independently, all three came to see the efficacy of Boolean-type logic for computer design.

While Shannon pondered at MIT, a physics professor named John Atanasoff was struggling with the problem at Iowa State College. In January 1938, after two years of puzzling over the optimal design for a computer, Atanasoff decided to base his machine on the binary rather than the decimal numbering system. He reached that conclusion somewhat reluctantly, since he feared that his students and other users of the machine might have considerable difficulty in making the transition from decimal to binary. But the simplicity of the two-numeral system, combined with the relative ease of representing two symbols instead of 10 in a computer's circuitry, seemed to Atanasoff to outweigh the stumbling block of unfamiliarity. In any case, the machine could make the conversions. By the fall of 1939, Atanasoff had built a rough prototype and was looking for financing to develop his computer further.

Across the country, meanwhile, George Stibitz, a research mathematician with Bell Telephone Laboratories, was spending odd moments at his self-professed habit of "thinking things up." One day in 1937, he realized that Boolean logic was a natural language for the circuitry of electromechanical telephone relays.

A TINKERER GOES TO WORK

Stibitz acted on this notion at once, certain that his employer would find use for whatever he came up with. He began by doing what tinkerers always do: He scrounged some parts. Working on his kitchen table in the evenings, he hooked together old relays, a couple of batteries, flashlight bulbs, wire, and metal strips cut from a tobacco can. The resulting device, using the logic of Boolean gates to control current flow, was an electromechanical circuit that could perform binary addition. It was the first of its kind in the United States. Today the binary adder circuit (pages 44-45) remains a basic building block of every digital computer.

Over the next couple of years, Stibitz and a Bell switching engineer named Samuel Williams developed a device that could subtract, multiply and divide as well as add complex numbers. Stibitz called his machine the Complex Number Calculator, and in January 1940, he set it to work at company headquarters in Manhattan. A teletype machine nearby transmitted signals to it and received answers from it within seconds. Two more teletypes were added in other parts of the building, allowing people in more than one location to use the same computer. Then, in September, a fourth teletype was set up 250 miles away in McNutt Hall at Dartmouth College in Hanover, New Hampshire. There, before an astonished audience of 300 members of the American Mathematical Society, Stibitz conducted a demonstration of remote-control electromechanical computation.

Yet even before Shannon wrote his thesis or Stibitz began tinkering on his kitchen table, a kindred soul in Berlin was building his own computating device in the cramped apartment he shared with his parents. As an engineering student in 1934, Konrad Zuse had come to loathe the long, boring mathematical calculations required by the profession. And like Leibniz before him, like Atanasoff, Shannon and Stibitz, Zuse began to dream of a machine that could take over the tiresome chore. Ideally, he thought, such a machine could be programmed to perform any mathematical task required, no matter how complex. Although he was unaware of the work of Charles Babbage, Zuse set out to design a general-purpose computer along the lines of Babbage's Analytical Engine *(page 13)*.

Zuse knew virtually nothing about calculating machines such as the differential analyzer. But decades later, he would note that this was actually an advantage: Because of his ignorance, he was free to go in new directions and to choose the best system for calculation. After experimenting with the decimal system, Zuse decided to use the simpler binary system instead.

BUILDING THE Z1

In 1936, Zuse quit his job at an engineering firm and plunged full-time into his project, backed by a little money from friends and using a small table in the corner of the family living room as a work space. As his machine took shape and grew, he pushed another table or two next to the original one to accommodate it. Eventually he moved his operations to the center of the room, and after two years he had completed an ungainly prototype that occupied seven square feet.

The Z1, as Zuse called his machine, was primarily mechanical. Binary digits, for example, were represented by pins in slotted metal plates; a pin at one end of a slot signified a one, at the opposite end, a zero. Other metal plates retrieved or stored data by sliding the pins back and forth. Input and output were equally simple. With paper tape unavailable, Zuse entered problems into the machine by means of holes punched in discarded movie film. Results of calculations were flashed on a board composed of many little light bulbs, among the Z1's few electrical components. Light bulbs and film were also incorporated in a successor machine, the Z2.

Zuse happily continued work on his machines until 1939. But worldwide war was coming. When the storm broke, Zuse, Stibitz and other computer pioneers on both sides of the Atlantic would be swept up into a desperate race to add their new kind of weapon to the modern arsenal. The war would spur other major advances in computer theory and design *(Chapter 3)*. And it also consolidated the gains of the long line of binary proponents stretching back to Leibniz: The two-symbol approach to expressing information would eventually be accepted as the computer's natural language.

Zeros and Ones: Simple Rules for a Complex World

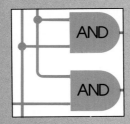

Although the internal language that governed some of the early computers was based on the decimal number system, virtually every computer since the 1950s has used binary instead. With only two symbols, the binary system makes for very efficient and much less costly circuitry. The microscopic electronic switches in a modern computer's central processor need assume only two states — on or off, representing zero and one — rather than the 10 needed for a decimal circuit. Binary's two-state characteristic also corresponds to the algebraic system of logic devised by the 19th Century British mathematician George Boole: A proposition is either true or false, just as a switch is either open or closed, or a binary digit is either one or zero.

When switches are arranged according to Boolean principles, they create circuits that can perform both mathematical and logical operations. Illustrated on page 44 is an arithmetic circuit called a binary adder. Adders do what their name implies: They add binary numbers, following rules similar to those for adding decimal numbers.

Computers are also called upon to deal with forms of information that do not, on their face, have anything to do with numbers or logic. For example, they can process sounds coming in through a microphone and reproduce them through speakers or onto special disks. They can monitor temperatures in laboratories or manipulate images on television. In these cases, the computer must first "digitize" the information — translate it into binary digits. To digitize music, for instance, the computer takes periodic measurements of the sound waves and records each measurement as a binary number (pages 48-49). By performing these measurements at precise and extremely short intervals, a computer can record the sound output of an entire symphony orchestra — and then reproduce the music with astonishing fidelity simply by reversing the digitizing process.

DECIMAL		BINARY			
PLACE	PLACE	PLACE	PLACE	PLACE	PLACE
10	1	8	4	2	1
	0				0
	1				1
	2			1	0
	3			1	1
	4		1	0	0
	5		1	0	1
	6		1	1	0
	7		1	1	1
	8	1	0	0	0
	9	1	0	0	1
1	0	1	0	1	0

Reading binary numbers. Because the system has only two symbols, binary place columns increase by powers of two and binary numbers quickly turn into multidigit figures. Adding up the value of places marked by binary 1s gives the decimal equivalent. Thus, binary 101 is one 4 plus one 1, for decimal 5.

From Decimal to Binary and Back

In the binary number system, as in the decimal, the value of a digit is determined by where it stands in relation to the other digits in a number. In decimal, a 1 by itself is worth 1; putting it to the left of two zeros makes the 1 worth 100. This simple rule is the backbone of arithmetic: Numbers to be added or subtracted, for example, are first arranged so that their place columns line up.

In decimal notation, each position to the left of the decimal point indicates an increased power of 10. In binary, or base 2, each place to the left signifies an increased power of two: 2^0 is one, 2^1 is two, 2^2 is four, and so on. As illustrated at left and on the opposite page, finding the decimal equivalent of a binary number is simply a matter of noting which place columns the binary 1s occupy and adding up their values. Conversion the other way — from decimal to binary — is shown below.

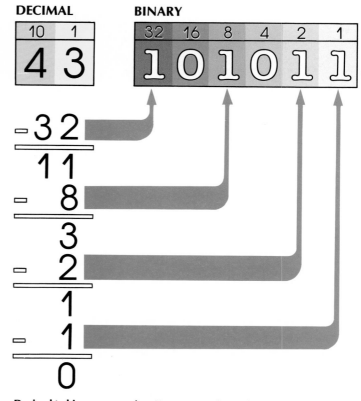

Decimal to binary conversion. To convert a decimal number to binary, first subtract the largest possible power of two, and keep subtracting the next largest possible power from the remainder, marking 1s in each column where this is possible and 0s where it is not. For decimal 43, there is one 32, no 16, one 8, no 4, one 2 and one 1 — resulting in the binary number 101011.

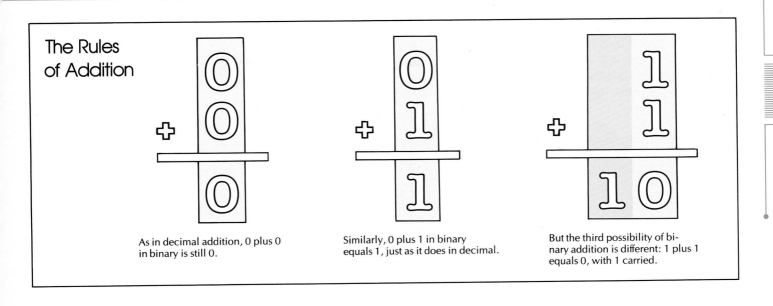

The Rules of Addition

As in decimal addition, 0 plus 0 in binary is still 0.

Similarly, 0 plus 1 in binary equals 1, just as it does in decimal.

But the third possibility of binary addition is different: 1 plus 1 equals 0, with 1 carried.

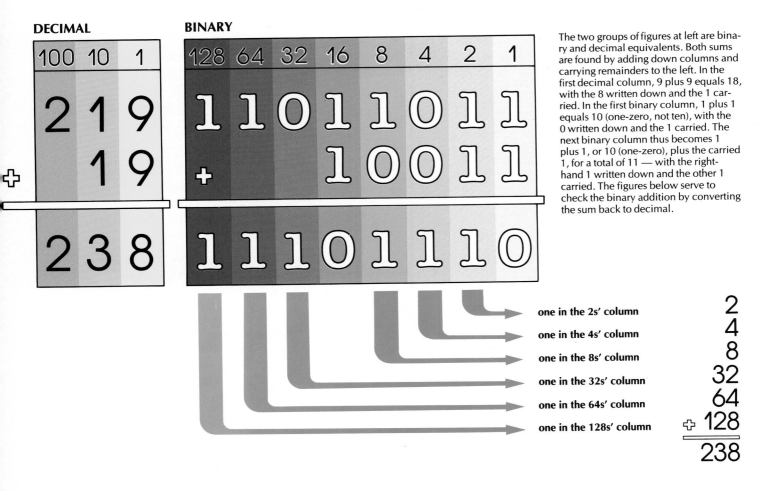

DECIMAL

100	10	1
2	1	9
	1	9
2	3	8

BINARY

128	64	32	16	8	4	2	1
1	1	0	1	1	0	1	1
			1	0	0	1	1
1	1	1	0	1	1	1	0

The two groups of figures at left are binary and decimal equivalents. Both sums are found by adding down columns and carrying remainders to the left. In the first decimal column, 9 plus 9 equals 18, with the 8 written down and the 1 carried. In the first binary column, 1 plus 1 equals 10 (one-zero, not ten), with the 0 written down and the 1 carried. The next binary column thus becomes 1 plus 1, or 10 (one-zero), plus the carried 1, for a total of 11 — with the right-hand 1 written down and the other 1 carried. The figures below serve to check the binary addition by converting the sum back to decimal.

one in the 2s' column

one in the 4s' column

one in the 8s' column

one in the 32s' column

one in the 64s' column

one in the 128s' column

$$
\begin{array}{r}
2 \\
4 \\
8 \\
32 \\
64 \\
+\ 128 \\
\hline
238
\end{array}
$$

Building Blocks of Logic

All modern computers employ a system of logic devised by George Boole. The thousands of microscopic electronic switches within a computer chip can be arranged into systems of "gates" that deliver logical — that is, predictable — results. The most fundamental logic gates, called AND, OR and NOT, appear at right. All other gates used in computers can be derived from these three.

Wired together in various combinations, logic gates enable the computer to perform its tasks with the coded pulses of its binary language. (For a look at the circuitry that physically accomplishes the work of a logic gate, see page 75.) Each logic gate accepts inputs in the form of high or low voltages, judges them by predetermined rules and produces a single, logical output expressed as either a high or a low voltage; the voltage represents any binary concept: yes-no, one-zero or TRUE-FALSE propositions. A simple AND gate, for example, passes on the equivalent of a binary 1 only if all inputs are 1, or logically TRUE.

The rules that govern logic gates enable them to regulate the movement of data and instructions within the computer. For example, certain data would move from one location to another only if a given AND gate receives TRUE signals on all the input lines channeled to it.

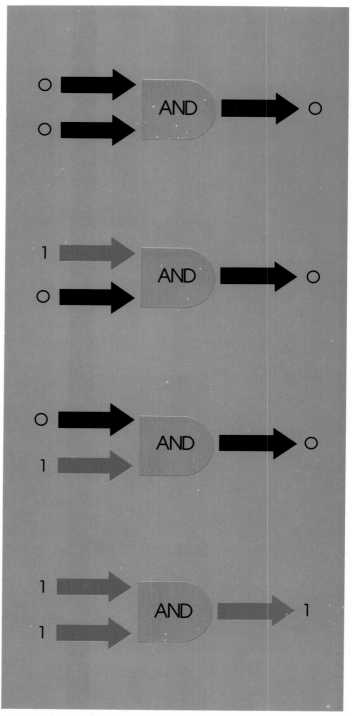

The gates pictured above represent AND gates, shaped according to the symbolic convention of electric circuitry. Although each gate is depicted with two input arrows, AND gates can in fact accept more than two inputs. Like all logic gates, however, they yield just one output. The fundamental rule of an AND gate is that it will deliver the equivalent of a binary 1, or logical TRUE, only if all its inputs are logically TRUE. The top three gates here yield 0, or FALSE, because none has 1s for both inputs; only the bottom gate can give 1, or TRUE, for its output.

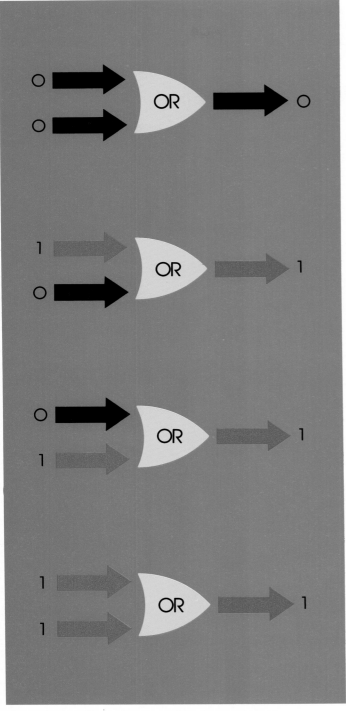

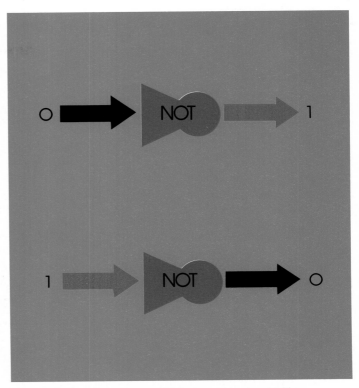

These circle-tipped triangles are NOT gates, or inverters. Unlike an AND or OR gate, a NOT gate accepts just one input, which it then reverses, turning 0s into 1s and 1s into 0s. NOT gates are often combined with AND gates and OR gates to form NAND, or "not and," and NOR, or "not or," gates. These hybrid devices process inputs by the usual AND/OR rules — and then automatically invert the output.

Like AND gates, OR gates can accept more than two inputs but can yield only one output. However, OR gates are less particular than AND gates. As illustrated here, an OR gate will deliver a binary 1 or logical TRUE if any one of its inputs is TRUE. The only time an OR gate yields the equivalent of binary 0 or logical FALSE is when all of its inputs are FALSE.

Linking the Logic Gates

The AND, OR and NOT gates shown on the preceding pages combine in various ways to form electronic circuits called half-adders *(below)* and full-adders *(opposite),* which enable the computer to perform binary addition. With adjustments, these ingenious devices can also be used for subtraction, multiplication and division.

The simpler of the two circuits, the half-adder, can sum two binary digits and pass on the result, with remainder. But it cannot accommodate a third digit, carried over from a previous sum, and thus typically is used only in the first position in a logical adding chain, where the ones column is certain to be free of another column's remainder. By contrast, a full-adder can handle two binary digits plus a carry and may be used anywhere in the chain.

These half-adders — each made of an OR, a NOT and two AND gates — demonstrate the addition of two binary digits. The top adder channels current from both the 1 and 0 inputs through both the OR gate and the first AND gate; the OR gate yields a 1, the AND a 0. The NOT gate then inverts the 0 to a 1, which joins the 1 from the OR gate as input to the second AND gate to produce a 1, with no remainder. The bottom adder follows the same procedure to add 1 and 1, with a 1 carried.

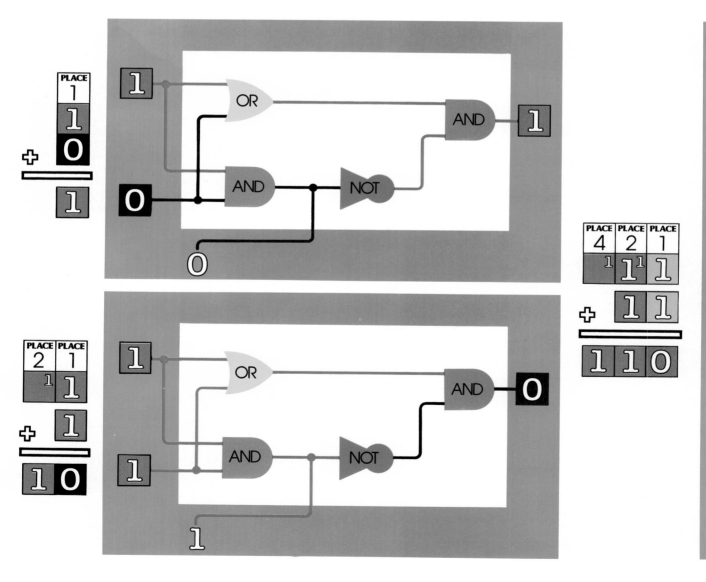

There is no one combination of logical elements that constitutes a proper half- or full-adder. The various gates can be set up in many different ways. (An OR gate by itself suffices for three fourths of what a half-adder does, since it yields a 0 when both inputs are 0 and a 1 when either input is a 1. Unfortunately, an OR gate also yields only a 1 when both inputs are 1, rather than 0 with 1 carried.) For all mathematical and logical purposes, it matters only that the arrangement delivers a 1 or a 0 when it should. The diagrams below illustrate two simple and straightforward schemes. Wires carrying high voltage, or binary 1, are red, those carrying low voltage, or binary 0, are black. Wiring intersections—places where current from one input is channeled to two or more different gates—are marked by dots.

A full-adder is needed to handle a carry-in generated by an addition in the rightmost column. In this example, the gates are arranged in three sections for clarity. The top section processes the carry-in and one of the inputs, yielding a 0, which passes to the last section for processing with the other input. This section then yields 1. The bottom section processes both inputs and the carry-in, to yield a 1, which passes to the carry-out line.

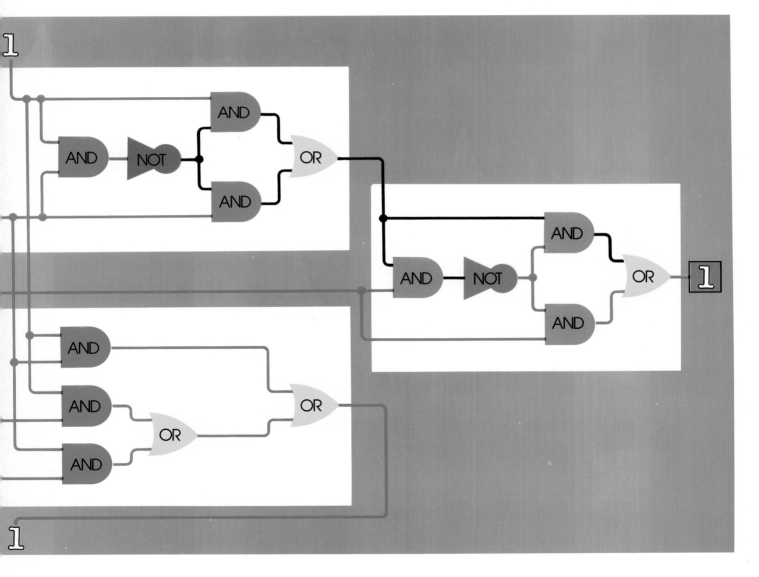

A Cascade of Adders

Just as logic gates combine into adders, so individual adders can be linked together to form something called a cascading adder — a device with one adder for each pair of bits in the problem. In the example below, two four-bit numbers (*right*) are summed by a cascade of four adders. The first one is a half-adder for the lowest-order bits, which can generate but never receive a carry digit. All the others are full-adders. Arrays like this can be extended to add binary numbers of whatever length the system has been designed to use.

Adding equivalent binary and decimal numbers produces equivalent results, including carries to the next column. Just as 7 equals binary 0111, and 6 equals binary 0110, so the sum of 7 and 6 — 13 — equals the sum of 0111 and 0110, or binary 1101.

PLACE 8	PLACE 4	PLACE 2	PLACE 1	
0	1	1	1	7
0	1	1	0	+6
1	1	0	1	13

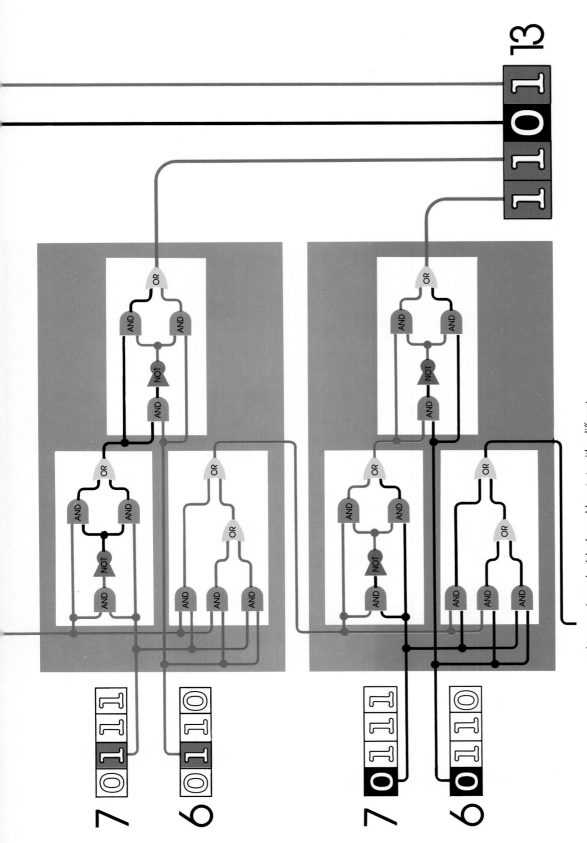

7 [0111]
6 [0110]

7 [0111]
6 [0110]

[1110]
[1101] 13

In this cascade, each of the four adders starts with a different set of inputs. The half-adder at top adds 1 and 0 to get 1, with no carry. The first full-adder sums two 1s for 0, carry 1. The next full-adder adds two 1s and the previous adder's carry to get 1, carry 1. The last adder combines a pair of 0s and a carry to get 1. The result: 1101, or 13. In each case where a carry was generated, it fell out, or cascaded down, to the next adder.

Music by the Numbers

Like all sound, music is made up of waves of compressed air that cause vibrations upon striking the eardrum or the diaphragm of a microphone. In a microphone for amplifying or for recording, the moving diaphragm modulates an electric current to create an analog of the sound. That is, the diaphragm generates currents whose voltage fluctuations correspond to the pressure fluctuations of the sound waves. Conventional recording devices store the wave pattern on magnetic tape or as a grooved track on a record. But during the recording process, variations in the power supply and in temperature can affect the shape of the wave pattern, diminishing the accuracy of the reproduction.

With the advent of so-called digital recording, the on-off simplicity of the binary code is used to achieve near-perfect fidelity to live sound. By a process called "sampling and quantization," a digital recording device turns a microphone's output into coded pulses of electricity. At the rate of thousands of times per second, one circuit in the recording device freezes, or samples, the voltage being generated by the microphone; another circuit measures the sample and gives it a decimal value, which is then translated into binary form. Reproducing the wave pattern is then simply a matter of converting the binary numbers back to precise voltages, which drive the speakers of the sound system.

On a digital record such as this compact disk, the information (sound) is carried by concentric circles of pits and spaces (left). The laser beam in a compact-disk player reads the pits as zeros and the reflecting spaces as ones. Electronic circuitry eventually reconverts this stream of digits into music, in a series of steps like those illustrated below.

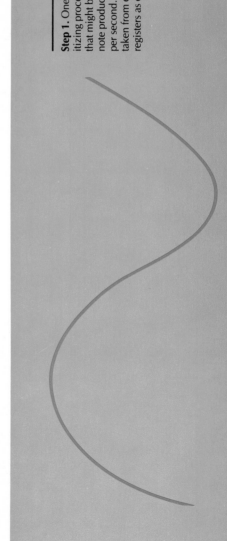

Step 1. One cycle of a sound wave is the starting point for the digitizing process, simplified here for clarity. The wave shown is one that might be formed by a pure note—middle C, for example, the note produced by a tuning fork set to vibrate at the rate of 262 cycles per second. To make a digital recording, 172 samples would be taken from each of the wave cycles. As shown below, each sample registers as electric voltage measured in decimal units.

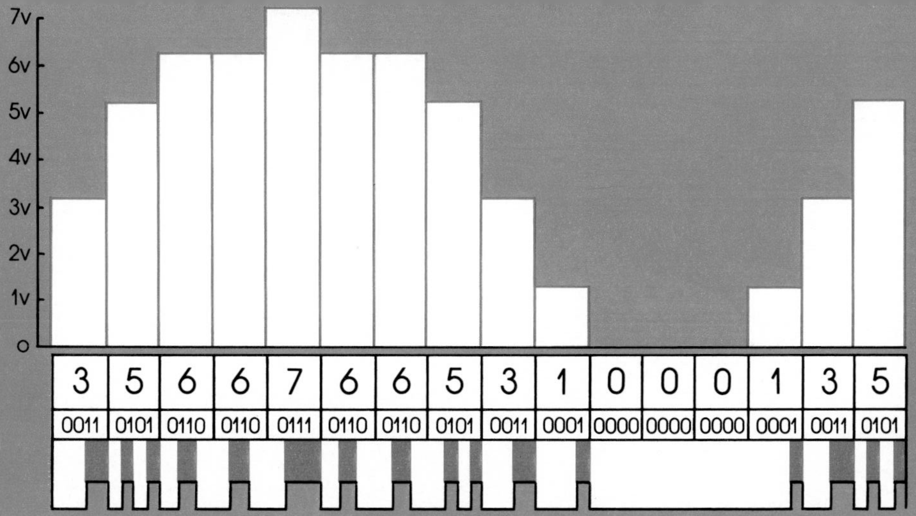
7v
6v
5v
4v
3v
2v
1v
0
3 5 6 6 7 6 6 5 3 1 0 0 0 1 3 5
0011 0101 0110 0110 0111 0110 0110 0101 0011 0001 0000 0000 0000 0001 0011 0101

Step 2. A total of 262 times 172, or 45,064, samples are taken every second from each stereo channel. Only 16 of the 172 samples per cycle are illustrated here. The voltage of each sample is then measured by a so-called quantizing circuit, which matches the reading to a binary code. The code for each sample is usually 16 bits long; for simplicity, each binary "word" here is composed of four bits.

Step 3. After the samples have been quantized, or converted into the binary code, the bits are formed into something called a pulse train, with ones, or on, represented as raised segments in the graph and zeros, or off, represented as a flat line. This train of on-off electrical pulses guides the light beam of the recording laser, which engraves the digital information onto the disk in the form of pits and spaces.

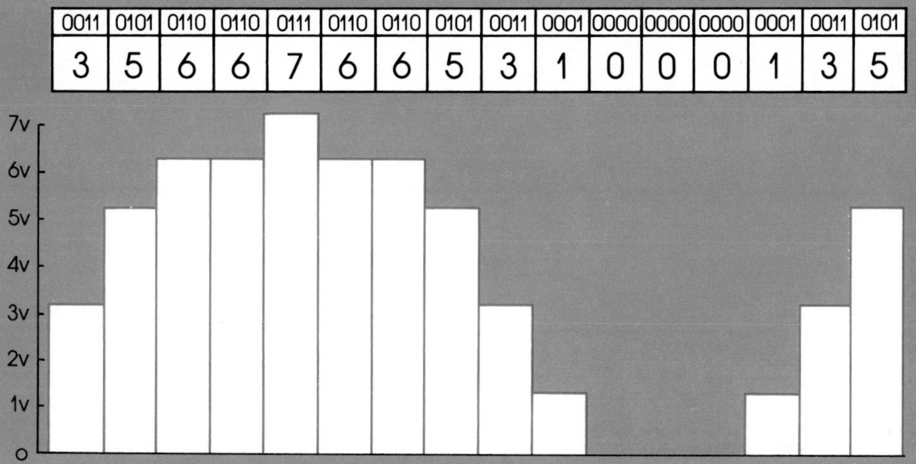
0011 0101 0110 0110 0111 0110 0110 0101 0011 0001 0000 0000 0000 0001 0011 0101
3 5 6 6 7 6 6 5 3 1 0 0 0 1 3 5
7v
6v
5v
4v
3v
2v
1v
0

Step 4. During playback, another laser, this one in the digital record player, reads the pits and spaces on the disk as the zeros and ones of the quantized code of the music. The numbers are then converted back into discrete voltage amplitudes.

Step 5. Finally, a special filter called an output-smoothing circuit blends the discrete steps of the voltage samples into a smooth wave that closely approximates the original. This filtered wave form, fed to the output amplifiers, is what the listener hears from the speakers.

A Wartime Burst
of Progress

Late in 1941, shortly after the United States entered World War II, the president of the International Business Machines Corporation sent a telegram to the White House. Like many other corporation executives in that time of national emergency, Thomas J. Watson Sr. offered to put the facilities of his company at the disposal of the government for the duration.

It was a sincere patriotic gesture but the shrewd old entrepreneur also knew he had little choice. All-out war meant an unprecedented mobilization of industry and science to make conventional weapons and to develop the technology for unconventional ones. Watson knew the government would take what it needed, and as his son Tom Jr. put it, he was "making a virtue out of necessity."

The IBM facilities that Watson volunteered seemed to have little to do with battle. They were geared to the office, turning out typewriters, desk calculators and tabulating machines of the type devised by Herman Hollerith in 1890. Watson, a 67-year-old former cash-register salesman, had built the company into a multimillion-dollar concern by combining a keen intuition for the most promising new technology with an evangelical fervor for selling. With signs and banners he exhorted his employees to "Think," and he insisted that they all wear neatly ironed white shirts. Furthermore, he demanded from them a kind of religious commitment. "You have to put your heart in the business," he liked to say, "and the business in your heart."

Switches like these — 420 of them in all — were set by hand to enter the constant values required for computations in decimal by the first program-controlled computer in the United States. Completed in 1943 and named the Mark I, this pioneering machine was sheathed in a streamlined case of glass and gleaming stainless steel, and stretched 51 feet across a laboratory room at Harvard University *(below)*.

True to Watson's pledge to the White House, IBM went to war. Thousands of tabulators — the giant punch card-sorting machines that would later be called data processors — helped untangle the snarls of paper work generated by full-scale mobilization. Watson even converted part of his manufacturing facilities to the production of bombsights and rifles.

But Watson had something else up his pristine white sleeve. Two years before the Japanese attack on Pearl Harbor, he had invested $500,000 of IBM's money in the audacious plan of a young Harvard mathematician named Howard Aiken. Aiken, who had been frustrated by the enormous number of calculations required for his doctoral dissertation, wanted to go beyond the sorters and calculators then available and build the kind of general-purpose programmable computers Charles Babbage had first envisioned.

The war sidetracked Aiken at first. Soon after Pearl Harbor, he was called to active duty in the Navy, where he distinguished himself by singlehandedly disarming a new type of German torpedo. But Watson quickly intervened with the authorities, touting the embryonic computer's potential for calculating the trajectories of cannon shells, and managed to get Aiken detached to special duty at IBM's plant in Endicott, New York.

BUILDING THE MARK I

With the Navy's blessing and IBM's money and engineering support, Aiken set to work building the machine out of untested 19th Century concepts and proven 20th Century technology. Babbage's original description of his Analytical Engine was a more than adequate guide. ("If Babbage had lived 75 years later," Aiken said afterward, "I would have been out of a job.") Simple electromechanical relays served as the on-off switching devices, and punched tape supplied instructions, or a program, for manipulating the data. The data itself was fed into the machine on punched cards, encoded in IBM's standard decimal format rather than in the binary number system used by John Atanasoff and George Stibitz for their machines.

The development of the Mark I, as the device came to be called, proceeded with remarkably few snags. Early in 1943 it was switched on for a successful test at Endicott, then shipped to Harvard, where it became the center of a series of clashes between the inventor and his patron.

Both Aiken and Watson were used to getting their own way. They clashed first over the appearance of the machine. Fifty-one feet long and eight feet high, the Mark I contained no fewer than 750,000 parts strung together with 500 miles of wire. It looked like an engineer's nightmare. Aiken wanted to leave the innards exposed so that interested scientists could inspect them. Watson, ever mindful of IBM's corporate image, insisted the machine be encased in glass and gleaming stainless steel.

Watson prevailed in this and other matters, but Aiken got his revenge when the Mark I was introduced to the press at Harvard in August 1944. He scarcely mentioned IBM's role in the project and said not a word about Tom Watson. Watson was furious. "You can't put IBM on as a postscript," he screamed at Aiken afterward. "I think about IBM just as you Harvard fellows do about your university." Watson's son and successor, Tom Jr., said later that "if Aiken and my father had had revolvers, they would both have been dead."

Shortly thereafter, Watson leased the machine to the Navy, which used it to solve difficult ballistics problems under Aiken's supervision. The Mark I could handle — or "crunch" — numbers up to 23 digits long. It could add or subtract them in ³⁄₁₀ of a second and multiply them in three seconds. Such speed, though only a little faster than Babbage had envisioned, was unprecedented. In a single day the machine could whip through calculations that formerly required a full six months.

The computer's modernistic image was carefully tended. Watson's glass and stainless steel helped, as did the spit and polish of the Navy officers who ran the machine. They marched around smartly, as one Harvard scientist recalled the scene, saluting each other and "appearing to operate the thing while at attention." Only the computer's noise marred this aura of efficiency. As the machine's 3,304 relays clicked open and shut to turn the assemblage of shafts and wheels, the incessant clatter reminded one observer of a "roomful of old ladies knitting away with steel needles."

The Mark I would continue its reverberant mathematical labors at Harvard for fully 16 years. Yet, in spite of its long and solid service, it was not the success that Tom Watson had hoped for. Other researchers — German and British as well as American — were pushing computers in more promising directions. In fact, the Mark I was obsolete before it was built.

Konrad Zuse led the way in Germany. In 1941, nearly two years before the Mark I crunched its first numbers, and soon after the development of his test models Z1 and Z2, Zuse completed an operational computer: a program-

Surrounded by an array of frames and pulleys, a sailor tends to the Mark I's voracious appetite for the punched paper tape that controlled the machine. After wartime duty computing complex ballistics tables, Mark I put in 15 more years at Harvard, cranking out mathematical tables and working on assorted projects ranging from economic modeling to computer circuit design.

controlled device based on the binary system. Designated the Z3, this machine was much smaller than Aiken's and vastly cheaper to build. It had to be. Though he had some help from the government, which released him from the Army after six months' service and gave him an engineering job in the aircraft industry, Zuse was still doing most of his computer work where he had begun it years earlier — in his parents' living room.

Both the Z3 and a successor, the Z4, were used to solve engineering problems of aircraft and missile design. Zuse also built several special-purpose computers, two of which helped evaluate the aerodynamic characteristics of wings and rudders on an unmanned, radio-controlled aircraft that saw limited service late in the war. But in one respect, Zuse's work was thwarted by the German government.

In 1942, he and his sometime associate Helmut Schreyer, an Austrian electrical engineer, had proposed constructing a radical kind of computer. The two men wanted to redesign the Z3 so that it used vacuum tubes rather than electromechanical relay switches. Unlike the electromechanical switches, vacuum tubes have no moving parts; they control the flow of current by electrical forces

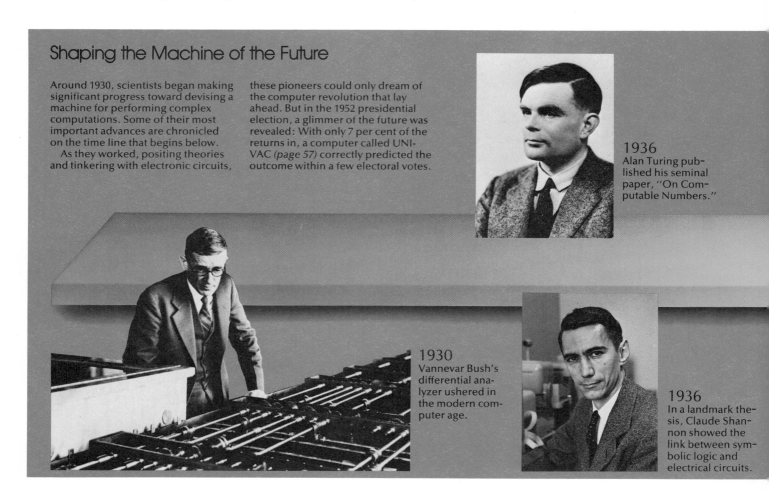

Shaping the Machine of the Future

Around 1930, scientists began making significant progress toward devising a machine for performing complex computations. Some of their most important advances are chronicled on the time line that begins below.

As they worked, positing theories and tinkering with electronic circuits, these pioneers could only dream of the computer revolution that lay ahead. But in the 1952 presidential election, a glimmer of the future was revealed: With only 7 per cent of the returns in, a computer called UNIVAC *(page 57)* correctly predicted the outcome within a few electoral votes.

1936
Alan Turing published his seminal paper, "On Computable Numbers."

1930
Vannevar Bush's differential analyzer ushered in the modern computer age.

1936
In a landmark thesis, Claude Shannon showed the link between symbolic logic and electrical circuits.

alone. The machine Zuse and Schreyer envisioned would have operated a thousand times faster than anything the Germans had at the time.

Their proposal was turned down. It was still early in the war, and Hitler felt so certain of quick victory that he had ordered an embargo on all but short-term scientific research. "They asked when the machines would work," Zuse recalled. "We said about two years. They said we would win the war by that time."

Among the potential uses Zuse and Schreyer had cited for their high-speed computer was breaking the codes the British used to communicate with commanders in the field. Neither man knew it at the time, but the British were developing just such a machine and for just such a purpose.

In contrast with Zuse's make-do operation in Berlin, the British project was going forward under the highest priority as part of a remarkable codebreaking effort known as *Ultra*. The *Ultra* project stemmed from a dazzling coup by the Polish secret service. Before the fall of their nation in 1939, the Poles had managed to create a replica of the German cipher-generating apparatus called Enigma and to smuggle it to the British, along with a description of how it worked.

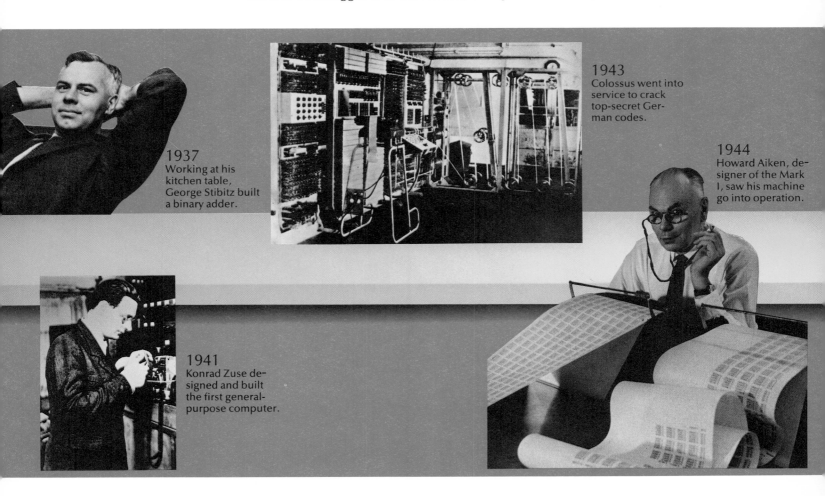

1937
Working at his kitchen table, George Stibitz built a binary adder.

1943
Colossus went into service to crack top-secret German codes.

1944
Howard Aiken, designer of the Mark I, saw his machine go into operation.

1941
Konrad Zuse designed and built the first general-purpose computer.

The Enigma device, an electromechanical teleprinter, scrambled messages by means of several spinning rotors. The sender would set the teleprinter to a particular key, plug in switchboard-like cords according to a predetermined pattern and type in the message to be sent; the machine then would automatically transmit the message in enciphered form. This much the Poles had been able to tell the British. But without the key and plug patterns—which the Germans changed three times a day—even another Enigma apparatus at the receiving end would be useless.

Hoping to penetrate the secrets of Enigma, British intelligence gathered a group of brilliant and eccentric researchers and sequestered them at Bletchley Park, a large Victorian estate near London. These so-called backroom boys ranged from engineers to professors of literature. Among them was a mathematician named Alan Turing.

A bold and original theoretician from Cambridge University, Turing was perhaps the strangest and certainly the most gifted of the lot — "a sort of scientific Shelley," a colleague once remarked. Long-haired and handsome, he wore rumpled clothes and espoused unconventional views, not denying,

1945
John von Neumann outlined the critical elements of a computer system.

1946
J. Presper Eckert and John Mauchly unveiled ENIAC, the first large-scale electronic digital computer.

for example, either his atheism or his homosexuality. He had a ''shrill stammer,'' his own mother admitted, ''and a crowing laugh which told upon the nerves even of his friends.''

Turing's idiosyncracies were legendary among the backroom boys. While at Cambridge, it was said, he had set his watch not by checking a clock or asking someone for the correct time but rather by sighting on a certain star, from a set spot, and then mentally calculating the hour. At Bletchley Park he often bicycled to work wearing a gas mask to ease his hay fever. Once Turing grew worried about the strength of the British pound. He melted down some silver coins and buried his lump of treasure on the Bletchley grounds — then promptly forgot where.

But Turing's genius was indisputable. In 1936, at the age of 24, he wrote what would later be recognized as a seminal paper in computer science. The paper focused on a rather abstruse problem in mathematical logic — the description of problems that are theoretically impossible to solve. In the process of trying to formulate such a description, Turing introduced a powerful, albeit imaginary, computing device that prefigured key characteristics of the modern computer.

1947
John Bardeen, William Shockley and Walter Brattain invented the transistor.

1952
Broadcast newsman Walter Cronkite used a UNIVAC computer to predict a presidential election.

1951
LEO, the first business computer, was completed.

Turing called his mechanical conceit a "universal machine" because it would be able to cope with every sort of legitimate — that is, solvable — problem, whether mathematical or logical. Data would be fed into the machine on a paper tape divided into squares, each square marked with a symbol or left blank. The machine would not only act upon these data squares but modify them as well, erasing and replacing the symbols in accordance with instructions stored in its internal memory.

Some of Turing's ideas eventually took shape in the machines built at Bletchley Park. First came a series of codebreaking devices employing electromechanical relays like those used by Konrad Zuse in Berlin, George Stibitz at Bell Labs and Howard Aiken at Harvard. These machines essentially worked by trial and error, scanning the combinations of symbols in the German code until some sort of sensible transliteration was discovered. But late in 1943 the backroom boys put into operation a far more ambitious series of machines. Instead of electromechanical relays, the new machines each used 2,000 vacuum tubes — the same technology and, coincidentally, about the same number of tubes that Zuse had proposed for the device he had not been allowed to develop. The British dubbed the new type of machine Colossus.

Intercepted enemy messages, thousands of them a day, were fed into Colossus in a manner similar to that envisioned by Alan Turing — as symbols punched on a loop of paper tape. The tape was fed into a photoelectric reader, which scanned it again and again, at the astonishing rate of 5,000 characters per second, comparing the ciphered message with known Enigma codes to find a match. Each machine had five such readers, enabling it to process an astounding 25,000 characters per second.

The work of the backroom boys at Bletchley Park was a collective effort, and Turing's precise role in designing Colossus and the other code-cracking instruments is still shrouded, almost half a century later, by the provisions of the British Official Secrets Act. "I won't say what Turing did made us win the war," said I. J. Good, a mathematician who served under him, "but I daresay we might have lost it without him."

Although its use of vacuum tubes represented a breakthrough in the development of the computer, Colossus was a special-purpose machine, limited to the

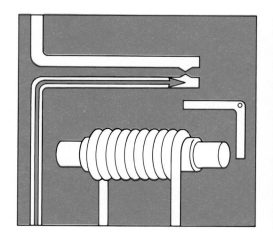
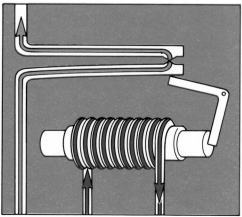

The earliest modern computers — the Mark I among them — relied heavily on electromechanical relay switches, then widely used in the telephone industry. When the switch was open (far left), no current flowed through the circuit. But when a low-voltage current (red) was passed through a coil wrapped around an iron bar (left), it created a magnetic field that attracted one end of an angled pivot. The other end of the pivot pressed two contact points together, closing the circuit and letting the current (green) proceed.

task of breaking codes. But across the Atlantic in Philadelphia, the requisites of war were giving rise to a device closer in spirit and function to Alan Turing's theoretical universal machine. The Electronic Numerical Integrator and Computer, or ENIAC, like Howard Aiken's Mark I, was born of the need to solve problems in ballistics. But ultimately it proved capable of tackling a wide variety of assignments.

GENESIS OF A UNIVERSAL COMPUTER

From the beginning of the war, the War Department's Ballistic Research Laboratory at the Army's Aberdeen Proving Ground in Maryland had labored to prepare artillery firing tables for gunners in the field. These tables were essential, enabling gun crews to adjust their aim according to the range and altitude of the target and under varying conditions of wind and temperature. But they required long and tedious strings of calculations — no fewer than 750 different multiplications for a single trajectory, with at least 2,000 trajectories per table. These calculations were speeded somewhat by the installation of a differential analyzer (page 54). But the device provided only approximate numbers, which had to be refined by platoons of human operators using ordinary desk calculators.

As the war effort speeded up, the laboratory fell increasingly behind schedule and enlisted help. It established an auxiliary computing system at the University of Pennsylvania's Moore School of Electrical Engineering. The school also had a differential analyzer, but two staff members at the school, John W. Mauchly and J. Presper Eckert, thought they could come up with something better.

Mauchly, a physicist with a special interest in meteorology, had long dreamed of a device that would allow him to apply statistical methods to weather forecasting. Before the war he had improvised simple digital counters that made use of vacuum tubes. But his interest in electronic computing may also have been stimulated by the work of John Atanasoff at Iowa State. During June of 1941, Mauchly spent five days at Atanasoff's home, where he saw a crude prototype of a 300-tube electronic computer being constructed by Atanasoff and his associate Clifford Berry.

Whatever Atanasoff's influence — and this would later become a matter of legal dispute — it was Pres Eckert who set Mauchly to work. Twelve years Mauchly's junior, Eckert was an engineering wizard who had built a crystal radio set on a pencil when he was only eight. As Mauchly said later, Eckert convinced him "that the things I was dreaming were possible."

In August 1942, Mauchly wrote a five-page memorandum outlining his and Eckert's proposal for a high-speed computer using vacuum tubes. He submitted it to the Moore School, where it was inadvertently misplaced. A few months later, however, the Army's technical liaison with the school, Lieutenant Herman Goldstine, happened to hear about the idea. By then the Army desperately needed new firing tables: Gunners were reporting from North Africa that the soft ground there caused unpredictable recoil of their cannon and threw off their aim. Goldstine, a mathematician at the University of Michigan before the war, immediately grasped the importance of the proposed computer and began to lobby on its behalf with his Army superiors. On April 9, 1943 — Eckert's 24th birthday — the Army awarded a $400,000 contract to the Moore School to build ENIAC.

The ENIAC team eventually grew to 50 people, with Mauchly as principal consultant and Eckert as chief engineer. In many ways, the two were very different, but they complemented each other. Mauchly, amiable and quick, spun off ideas; Eckert, reserved, cool and cautious, set rigorous standards to make sure the ideas would work. "He had a tremendous knack for being able to reduce things to a practical level, using simple engineering principles," a member of the ENIAC team said of Eckert. "Pres wasn't one to get lost in a myriad of equations."

The machine itself was fearsomely complicated — designed to have no fewer than 17,468 vacuum tubes. So many tubes were required because ENIAC handled numbers in decimal form. Mauchly preferred the familiar decimal approach because, he said, he wanted "the equipment to be readable in human terms." But such a large number of tubes, with their tendency to overheat and blow out, raised the specter of frequent breakdowns. With more than 17,000 tubes operating at the rate of 100,000 pulses per second, there were 1.7 billion chances every second of a tube failing. Eckert borrowed an idea from the big electric organs then used in theaters and ran the tubes at less than full voltage, reducing their failure rate to one or two a week.

Eckert also instituted a rigid program of quality control. Each of the more than 100,000 electronic components in the 30-ton machine had to be carefully tested. Then everything had to be just as carefully wired and soldered together — and sometimes resoldered — a monumental task that engaged even the cerebral Mauchly.

By late 1945, when ENIAC was finally assembled and ready for its first formal problem-solving test, the war for which it was built had ended. But the nature of that first test — calculations intended to evaluate the feasibility of the hydrogen bomb — pointed to the computer's continuing, or rather increasing, importance in the postwar and Cold War years.

ENIAC performed handsomely, processing approximately one million IBM punch cards in the course of the test. Two months later the machine was unveiled to the press. Eighteen feet high and 80 feet long, it was more than twice as large as Howard Aiken's Mark I. But that doubling of size was accompanied by a thousandfold increase in speed. ENIAC was "faster than thought," wrote an awestruck reporter.

THE VERSATILITY OF STORED PROGRAMS
Even as ENIAC went public, Mauchly and Eckert were at work designing the Army a successor. ENIAC's principal drawback was the difficulty in changing its instructions, or programs. The machine contained only enough internal memory to handle the numbers involved in the computation it was performing. This meant that the programs literally had to be wired into the complex circuitry. Someone who wanted to switch from calculating artillery firing tables to designing a wind tunnel had to scurry around the room like a crazed switchboard operator, unplugging and replugging hundreds of wires. Depending on the program's complexity, this job could take from four or five hours to two days — long enough to discourage anyone from using the machine for all-purpose computing.

ENIAC's successor — called EDVAC, for Electronic Discrete Variable Computer — was designed to speed things up by housing programs as well as data in its expanded internal memory. Rather than being wired into the circuitry, instructions would be stored electronically in a medium Eckert had come across while he was working on radar: a mercury-filled tube known as a delay line. Crystals in the tube generated acoustic pulses that bounced back and forth in the tube so slowly that they could effectively hold information in something like the way a canyon holds an echo. Equally significant, EDVAC would code information in binary rather than decimal form, substantially reducing the number of tubes required.

A QUICKSILVER GENIUS

Late in 1944, as Mauchly and Eckert wrestled with EDVAC and its stored-program concept, a special consultant appeared at the Moore School to help with the project. John von Neumann, then 41 and a giant among mathematicians, was to have a profound influence on the development of postwar computers.

Hungarian by birth, the son of a prosperous Jewish banker from Budapest, von Neumann was a product of the same intellectual milieu that had shaped such prominent physicists as Edward Teller, Leo Szilard, Dennis Gabor, Eugene Wigner and Oskar Jászi. Johnny (as all who knew von Neumann called him) was the brightest of the group. At six he could joke with his father in Classical Greek; at eight he mastered calculus. In his twenties, while teaching in Germany, he made important contributions to quantum mechanics, the cornerstone of nuclear physics, and developed the theory of games, a method of analyzing interactions among people that would find application in a range of disciplines from economics to military strategy. All his life he delighted in amazing his friends and students by performing difficult computations in his head, always faster than they could do the same work with paper, pencil and reference books. When he did use such mortal aids as blackboards, he filled them and erased them so quickly that a colleague looked up at the end of one von Neumann demonstration and said, "I see. Proof by erasure."

Eugene Wigner, a friend from his school days and himself a Nobel laureate, described von Neumann's mind as "a perfect instrument whose gears were machined to mesh accurately to a thousandth of an inch." Still, the perfection was leavened by a large measure of genial and rather endearing eccentricity. Von Neumann possessed a photographic memory, yet could not find the drinking glasses in a house he had occupied for 17 years. While traveling, he sometimes became so absorbed in mathematics that he had to call his office to find out why he had taken the trip in the first place.

Moreover, von Neumann enjoyed the full complement of human vanities. He dressed more like a Wall Street banker than a professor and took pains to cultivate people in power. He liked attractive women, good food and gadgets of all kinds, especially automobiles — which he cracked up at the rate of nearly one a year. But what he loved most, next to work, were the lavish parties he threw at his home in Princeton, New Jersey, where he was a fellow at the prestigious Institute for Advanced Study. On such occasions he gladly and jealously occupied center stage, holding forth on the genealogy of European royal families, recalling from memory entire passages of books he had read years before or reciting from his legendary store of off-color limericks.

Von Neumann moved so comfortably among his many social and professional worlds, shifting so effortlessly from abstract mathematical theory to the engineering components of computers, that some of his colleagues thought of him as the scientist's scientist — the kind of "new man" his name signified in German. Edward Teller once wryly praised him as "one of those rare mathematicians who could descend to the level of the physicist." For his part, von Neumann dismissed his quicksilver mobility with a joke, saying that "only a man born in Budapest can enter a revolving door behind you and come out in front."

Von Neumann's interest in computers stemmed in part from his involvement with the top-secret *Manhattan Project* at Los Alamos, New Mexico, where he had proved mathematically the soundness of the so-called implosive method of detonating the atomic bomb. Now he was contemplating the far more powerful hydrogen bomb, a weapon whose design and construction entailed a prodigious amount of calculation.

But he also saw that the computer could be much more than a high-speed calculator — that it was, at least potentially, an all-purpose tool for scientific research. In June 1945, less than a year after joining Mauchly and Eckert, von Neumann prepared a 101-page memorandum synthesizing the team's plans for EDVAC. This document, titled "First Draft of a Report on EDVAC," was a masterly analysis that stepped back from vacuum tubes and wiring diagrams to outline the computer's formal, logical organization. As the title indicated, von Neumann meant his paper as a preliminary version for internal review. But through a series of administrative errors by Army liaison officer Herman Goldstine and a new stenographer, copies of the memo were distributed to scientists in the United States and Great Britain.

Thanks to this informal publication, von Neumann's "First Draft" became the first document on electronic digital computers to be widely circulated — shared not only among co-workers but among laboratories, universities and countries as well. Scientists took particular note of it because of von Neumann's great prestige. His memo in effect gave scientific legitimacy to the computer. To this day, in fact, scientists sometimes refer to computers as "von Neumann machines" *(page 63)*.

Readers of the "First Draft" tended to assume that all the ideas in it, especially the critical proposal to store programs in the computer's memory, had originated with von Neumann himself. Few realized that Mauchly and Eckert had been talking about stored programs for at least six months before von Neumann came aboard, or that Alan Turing had incorporated an internal memory in his vision of a universal machine back in 1936. (Von Neumann in fact had known Turing and read his classic paper when Turing had spent time in Princeton just before the war.)

Mauchly and Eckert were outraged by the attention lavished on von Neumann and his "First Draft." Military secrecy had prevented them from publishing papers about their work, and now Goldstine had breached security and given the public platform to this newcomer. Eckert's resentment of Goldstine went so deep that more than three decades later he would not be caught in the same room with his former colleague. It was not just a matter of ego. Mauchly and Eckert clearly foresaw the commercial possibilities of their work, and they feared that the publication of von Neumann's memo would compromise their ability to obtain patents.

As it happened, arguments over the patent rights for ENIAC, not EDVAC, led to the eventual breakup of the Moore School team. School administrators insisted that individuals should not benefit financially from research carried out there. Von Neumann professed to agree (though he later unsuccessfully sought patents connected with EDVAC), but Mauchly and Eckert balked. On March 31, 1946, six weeks after the public unveiling of ENIAC, they rejected an ultimatum that they renounce all patent rights deriving from their work at the school. They quit and went into business for themselves.

SPARKING THE COMPETITION

But the pair helped write an ironic postscript. That summer they returned briefly to the Moore School to deliver a series of well-attended lectures on the electronic computer. One member of the audience, a British scientist named Maurice Wilkes, was particularly intrigued by their description of the stored program planned for EDVAC. He went home to Cambridge University and in 1949 — two years before the completion of EDVAC itself by what remained of the Moore School team—finished building one of the world's first stored-program computers: EDSAC, or Electronic Delay Storage Automatic Calculator.

This successful incorporation of the stored-program concept marked the final major step in the series of breakthroughs inspired by the war. The stage was now set for a postwar proliferation of ever-faster computers with an ability to

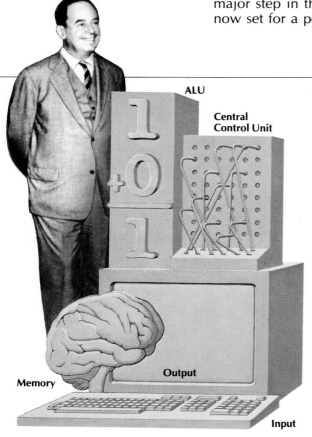

ALU

Central Control Unit

Memory

Output

Input

Blueprint for a Computer's Architecture

In a landmark memorandum published in 1945, Hungarian-born mathematician John von Neumann laid out in detail the five key components of what is often called the "von Neumann architecture" of the modern computer. To be both efficient and general-purpose, he wrote, a computing system must have a central arithmetic logic unit (ALU), a central control unit to orchestrate operations, a memory, an input unit and an output unit. He also noted that such a system should work with binary numbers, operate electronically rather than mechanically and perform its operations one at a time.

Commonplace today only because they have been so widely applied since von Neumann's time, these principles guided the design of the early mainframe computers as well as the smaller machines that have followed.

retrieve programs instantly from memory and to process not only ballistics or codes but information of every conceivable kind.

The computer era had dawned, but what of the peacetime fate of the men whose ingenuity and vision, blossoming under the pressures of war, had ushered in the new age?

Konrad Zuse lost all of his machines except Z4 in the Allied bombing of Berlin. To avoid capture by the Soviet Army during the last days of the war, he joined a convoy of rocket scientists and fled into the Bavarian Alps, hauling Z4 in a wagon. The U.S. Army quickly recruited one of the other scientists in the convoy, rocket specialist Wernher von Braun. But by then Zuse had stashed his machine in the cellar of a Bavarian farmhouse, and no one paid much attention to him. In 1949, Zuse began manufacturing commercial successors to the Z4. The business prospered, but it was nearly two decades before historians accorded Zuse and his homemade machines their rightful place in the evolution of the computer.

Alan Turing helped design one powerful postwar computer—a machine that incorporated a stored program and other ideas he had envisioned for his universal machine; the pilot model of ACE, or Automatic Computing Engine, became operational in May of 1950. He might have accomplished more, but his eccentricities kept getting in the way. Turing grew increasingly preoccupied with abstract questions about machine intelligence (he even devised a test to determine whether computers can actually think) and with his own pressing personal problems. His open homosexuality led to an arrest in 1952 for "gross indecency," and a sentence of psychoanalysis and hormone treatments. Two years later, while playing what he called the "desert island" game, in which he manufactured chemicals out of common household substances, Turing made potassium cyanide and then killed himself with it. He was 41 years old.

John von Neumann, joined at the Institute for Advanced Studies by Herman Goldstine from the Moore School team, collaborated on a number of computers of advanced design, beginning with the so-called IAS computer. Notable for its rapid intake of data, the IAS machine inspired a score of imitators, including the playfully dubbed "MANIAC"—for Mathematical Analyzer, Numerator, Integrator, and Computer—at Los Alamos. Von Neumann also served as a member of the Atomic Energy Commission and as chairman of the Air Force's advisory committee on ballistic missiles. He was privy to so much highly classified information that in 1957, as he lay in Walter Reed Hospital in Washington, D.C., dying of bone cancer at the age of 54, the Air Force surrounded him with medical orderlies specially cleared for security. His brilliant mind was breaking down under the stress of excruciating pain, and the Pentagon feared that he might start babbling military secrets.

John Mauchly and Presper Eckert started their own company in a former dance studio in Philadelphia and set out to create a general-purpose computer for commercial use: UNIVAC, the Universal Automatic Computer, an electronic stored-program machine that received its instructions on high-speed magnetic tape instead of punch cards. In 1950, a year before their first UNIVAC became operational at the U.S. Census Bureau, the partners ran out of money and sold their company to Remington Rand, a longtime manufacturer of electric shavers and punch-card tabulators. (As it turned out, another machine beat UNIVAC to the title of world's first commercial computer: LEO—for Lyons' Electronic Office—went into action calculating the weekly payroll for Lyons, a chain of English tearooms, a few months before UNIVAC's debut.) Neither Mauchly nor Eckert profited greatly from their contributions to the development of the electronic computer: Over a 10-year period each received about $300,000 from the sale of their company and from royalties on their ENIAC patents. The unkindest cut of all came in 1973, when a federal court invalidated those patents. Mauchly and Eckert had not invented the automatic electronic digital computer after all, the judge ruled, but had derived the concept from John Atanasoff—mainly during Mauchly's five-day visit to Iowa back in 1941. (Atanasoff never did complete an operational version of his computer, even though he spent the war working as an engineer in Naval Ordnance.) Mauchly denied any debt to Atanasoff and remained bitter about the matter until his death in 1980.

Howard Aiken stayed at Harvard to develop second, third and even fourth generations of his Mark I—but without the support of IBM. Tom Watson was so enraged by Aiken's failure to acknowledge the company's true role in the Mark I that he ordered his own researchers to construct a faster machine, thus propelling IBM into the computer business literally with a vengeance. By the time of Watson's death in 1956 at the age of 82, IBM had overtaken the sales lead established by Remington Rand with Mauchly and Eckert's highly successful UNIVAC.

IBM and computers soon became so synonymous in the public mind that most Americans assumed the company had invented the things in the first place. But that was insufficient balm; Watson's institutional heirs at IBM never forgot Aiken's insult. A quarter of a century after the completion of the Mark I, at an IBM-sponsored exhibit on the history of computers, IBM chairman T. V. Learson came upon the obligatory photograph of Howard Aiken. He stopped, muttered ''the sonofabitch,'' and walked on.

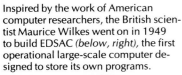

Inspired by the work of American computer researchers, the British scientist Maurice Wilkes went on in 1949 to build EDSAC (*below, right*), the first operational large-scale computer designed to store its own programs.

Evolution of the Microchip

On July 1, 1948 — two and a half years after the public unveiling of ENIAC, the world's first large-scale digital computer — a brief news story appeared on page 46 of *The New York Times*. The item reported the invention of a new gadget, "a device called a transistor, which has several applications in radio where a vacuum tube ordinarily is employed." Although the hindsight of later years would hail the transistor as perhaps the most important invention of the century, few people at the time recognized its significance. The *Times'* report was buried in its "News of Radio" section, bringing up the tail end of such items as the announcement by NBC that it would broadcast *Waltz Time* on Friday nights.

The story said nothing about the device's possible relationship to computers such as ENIAC, a subject that still generated front-page interest. Yet that little transistor — a pinhead-sized piece of a material called germanium encased in a sleek metal cylinder one-half inch long — would set electronics on the road to such extraordinary miniaturization that today's engineers could, if they wished, compress the entire circuitry of ENIAC onto a panel no larger than a playing card.

Transistors serve as the very nerve cells of today's computers. They do so by virtue of their speed and reliability in switching or amplifying currents. By blocking electric current or allowing it to pass (off-on), or by boosting a small voltage above a given threshold (low-high), they enable a computer circuit to express the two-state language that underlies all modern electronic information processing.

Earlier machines, such as the ones built by Konrad Zuse in Germany and by Howard Aiken at Harvard, had used electromechanical relays *(page 58)* to switch current on and off. Relays were soon supplanted in computers by vacuum tubes, which spoke the on-off language much more swiftly. Unlike relays with their noisy clicking, vacuum tubes — the product of decades of development that began with the tinkerings of Thomas Alva Edison in 1883 — had no moving mechanical parts. Within their airless precincts, all action was electronic.

The basic tube used in computers was known as a triode, for its three key

Stripped of its cover, an integrated circuit, or chip — the building block of modern computers — lies exposed in its packaging. The silicon chip, scarcely as large as a baby's fingernail, is tied to electrical contact points by gold wires finer than human hair.

A Switch Genealogy

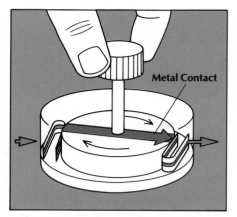

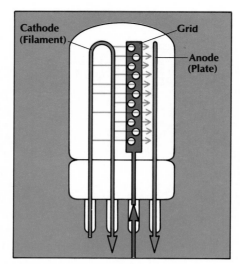

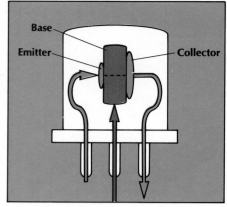

19th Century. Mechanical turn switch: This device provides a model for the operation of the electronic switches used in modern computers. Activated by a simple twisting motion, this basic switch goes into the on position when the metal contact element *(red)* is rotated to close the circuit between contact points, allowing current *(green)* to continue. Other types of switches look considerably different *(right)*, but their function is the same.

1906. Triode electron tube: Also called vacuum tubes, many thousands of these devices were required to run early computers. A positive charge to the grid encourages negatively charged electrons to surge across the vacuum between the cathode (a wire filament) and the anode (a metal plate), completing a circuit and enabling current to pass through. When negatively charged, the grid repels electrons and keeps the circuit broken.

1948. Junction transistor: In this pea-sized switch, current is turned on and off by the interaction of three specially treated, or "doped," layers of germanium. The emitter and the collector are doped to provide extra electrons, the base to provide extra "holes," or positive charge carriers. A positive charge *(red)* to the base enables electrons and holes to move; the electron carries current *(green)* from the emitter to the collector to complete the circuit.

elements: a cathode, which emitted negatively charged atomic particles called electrons when heated by an external power source; an anode, which collected these electrons after they had passed across an airless gap; and an intervening grid to control the flow *(above)*.

In addition to working as a switch (a negative charge to the grid repelled electrons flowing from the cathode), the triode served two other functions. Because it let current travel in only one direction, it acted as a rectifier, converting alternating current to direct current; this characteristic enabled the triode, when linked to an antenna, to detect radio waves. Equally significant, the triode could function as an amplifier: A small increase in the electrical signal fed to the grid brought a much larger increase in the charge received by the anode.

Nonetheless, vacuum tubes had numerous shortcomings: They took up space, gobbled electricity, generated heat and burned out rapidly. Nowhere were these disadvantages more dramatically illustrated than in the monstrous ENIAC, whose 17,468 tubes gave off so much heat that, despite fans intended to cool the machine, the temperature in the room sometimes soared to 120° F. Tubes, wrote one historian, "afflicted the early computers with a kind of technological elephantiasis." Clearly, without the development of a new kind of switch, the computer would remain enormous, unwieldly and too expensive for anyone but the government and big corporations to buy and maintain.

THE SEARCH FOR SOMETHING BETTER
By the time large-scale electronic computers made their debut in the 1940s, the communications industry was already looking for an alternative to bulky, fragile vacuum tubes as amplifiers. Research centered on a class of crystalline mineral materials known as semiconductors.

At the turn of the century, one of those minerals, galena (lead sulfide), had played a key role in radio sets. The contact formed between a crystal of galena and a metal wire as thin as a cat's whisker acted as a rectifier and could thus

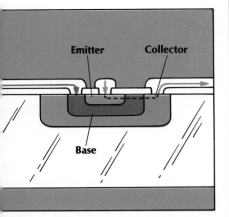

959. Planar transistor: Identical in principle to the junction transistor at left, the planar transistor is a mere 1/200 of an inch long. As shown in this cross-sectional view, a positive electric charge to the base permits passage of current from the emitter to the collector. The planar process allowed dozens of transistors, together with resistors and capacitors, to be formed all at the same time on one side of a silicon chip.

detect radio signals. For a brief period, the cat's whisker rectifier was the only useful radio detector available. The crystal device was unreliable, however, and vacuum tubes, which had the additional ability to amplify signals, eventually replaced the cat's whisker rectifier in radio sets.

But World War II — and the military's growing reliance on radar — revived the earlier receiving system. Radar requires the detection of extremely high-frequency signals, and the vacuum tube was too slow to rectify those frequencies accurately. Researchers went back to the cat's whisker and found that devices made of a fine wire attached to semiconductors such as silicon and germanium worked splendidly. This finding accelerated broader research into semiconductors; in the United States alone, at least three dozen laboratories were involved.

Physicists already knew some important things about the atomic structure and electronic properties of solids. They knew, for example, that the electrical conductivity of a substance depends on how tightly an atom's nucleus holds on to its outermost electrons. Most metals are good conductors because they contain an abundance of electrons that are not tightly bound and thus can be attracted to a positive charge or repelled by a negative one. Moving electrons are the carriers of electric current. Insulating substances such as rubber, on the other hand, fail to conduct electricity because their electrons are not so free to respond to electrical stimuli; they remain tightly bound to their atoms.

Semiconductors, whose properties were not completely understood at the start of the war, behave in yet another way. The atoms of semiconductor crystals are arrayed in a lattice, with electrons forming chemical bonds among them. In their pure state, semiconductors act more or less like insulators and will conduct electricity very poorly, if at all. But if a few atoms of certain other elements are introduced into the crystal lattice, the situation changes dramatically.

In some cases, the impurity introduces atoms whose bonding with the semiconductor atoms results in an extra electron; this excess of electrons gives the semiconductor a negative charge. In other cases, the contamination results in so-called holes, places in the bonds where an electron could fit if one were available; this lack of sufficient electrons gives the semiconductor a positive charge. Under the right circumstances, the semiconductor becomes capable of conducting current. Unlike metal conductors, however, semiconductors can conduct current in two ways. A negatively charged semiconductor will seek to dispose of its extra electrons, producing n-type (for negative) conduction. The current is carried by electrons. A positively charged substance, however, will seek a free electron to fill its extra hole. But as the hole is filled, another one is left by the vacating electron; in effect, the hole is a positive charge moving in the opposite direction from the electrons. Moreover, in either type of semiconductor, the so-called minority carriers — that is, electrons in p-type and holes in n-type — conduct current in the opposite direction from the majority carriers, a characteristic that was neglected and misunderstood for some time.

By the late 1930s, investigators had demonstrated that semiconductors, like vacuum tubes, could act as rectifiers. But until the intensive radar-related research during the war, no one understood how to control semiconductors well enough to make them predictable and practical as switches or amplifiers. Through that research, physicists developed much more reliable methods of "doping," or contaminating, crystals of germanium and silicon to create semiconductors with the desired electrical charge. For example, introducing minute amounts of phosphorus creates extra free electrons and produces n-type conduction. Doping the crystal with boron results in an excess of holes and produces p-type conduction.

At AT&T's Bell Laboratories and elsewhere, scientists who had taken part in this wartime effort were convinced that semiconductors had a bright future. AT&T had a pressing need for devices to replace the vacuum tubes and electro-mechanical relays that functioned as amplifiers and switches in the nationwide telephone system. In the summer of 1945, just before the end of the war, Bell mobilized its enormous resources and launched a major effort in the field of solid-state physics. Two key members of the team of physicists assigned to study semiconductors were Walter Brattain, a veteran of 16 years as a Bell experimentalist, and John Bardeen, a brilliant young theoretician new to the company.

The team's leader — and its strongest personality — was William Shockley, then 35 years old. The son of a mining engineer, Shockley was born in London but had grown up in Palo Alto, California. Although regarded as something of a showman, he was intensely serious and competitive. From the beginning of the Bell project, he was acutely aware of similar research being done at Purdue University.

Shockley brought to the project more than a decade of interest in semiconductors. Perhaps more important, he also brought a knack for reducing a research problem to its simplest elements and then pointing experiments in the right direction. On this occasion, however, his particular approach to making an amplifier, while valid in theory, failed to work in the initial tests. But as Bardeen and Brattain investigated the reasons for the failure, they were inspired to take a new experimental tack. They worked with a crystal of n-type germanium soldered to a metal disk. Pressed to the germanium, only $2/1,000$ of an inch apart, were the tips of two fine lines of gold foil, forming, in effect, two cat's whisker wires. A third metal contact, attached to the metal-and-germanium base, formed a common ground. On December 23, 1947, the two researchers applied an audio signal, modified, or biased, by a small positive voltage, to one gold contact, which acted as the emitter. The other gold contact, biased with a much larger negative voltage, acted as the collector. The result was an amplification — by a factor of about 50 — of the signal measured at the collector.

After nearly three years of research at an estimated cost of a million dollars, Bell had its semiconductor amplifier. The device's success suggested that positive charges, or holes, introduced into the germanium at the emitter flowed across the surface of the germanium to the collector, adding to the collector current. Because it transferred current across a resistor — that is, in a normally resistant direction — the device was first named transresistor, which was quickly shortened to transistor. A streamlined version introduced to the public six months later stirred little interest in *The New York Times* or other newspapers. Even the scientists at Bell were not completely satisfied with the first transistor, which was known as the point-contact model. The unpredictable device seemed bedeviled, Shockley wrote later, by "mysterious witchcraft."

Perhaps to compensate for not having shared directly in its invention, Shockley immediately set out to design experiments to explain the surface phenomena of the point-contact transistor. In a matter of days, he worked out much of the theory

70

for what would prove to be not merely an experiment but a transistor in its own right — and a better one at that. But perfecting it required so much persistence that a colleague admiringly referred to the device as the "persistor."

DEBUT OF THE JUNCTION TRANSISTOR

In 1951 Shockley presented the world with the first reliable junction transistor, a kind of three-layer germanium sandwich enclosed in a metal case that stood a half inch high. In what later became the most common form of this transistor — the so-called npn variety — a thin layer of p-type semiconductor is sandwiched between two layers of n-type material. One layer of n-type serves as the emitter, the other as the collector; the p-type layer in the middle is the base.

At the two junctions — between the emitter and the base, and between the base and the collector — a complex exchange of electrons and holes peculiar to semiconductors takes place. This exchange creates so-called depletion areas on either side of the junctions. When the transistor is at rest, the depletion area is too wide to allow current to flow across the junctions from emitter to collector. But when the n-layers are made sufficiently negative relative to the p-layer, the depletion area shrinks and current will flow. Moreover, a very small controlling

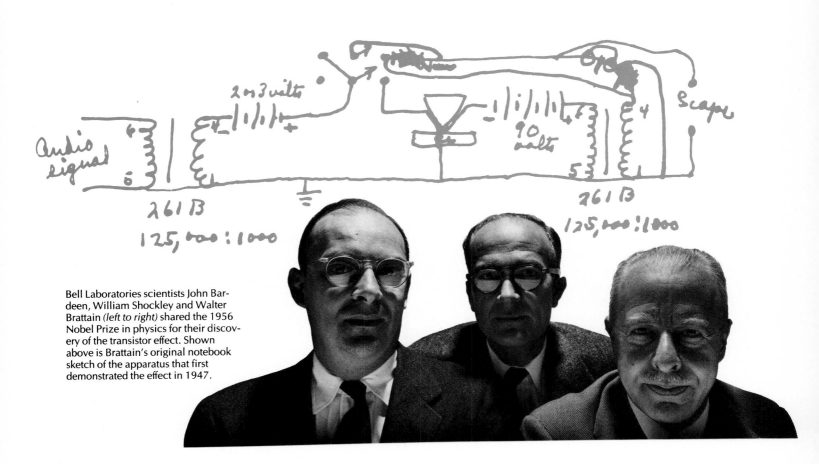

Bell Laboratories scientists John Bardeen, William Shockley and Walter Brattain *(left to right)* shared the 1956 Nobel Prize in physics for their discovery of the transistor effect. Shown above is Brattain's original notebook sketch of the apparatus that first demonstrated the effect in 1947.

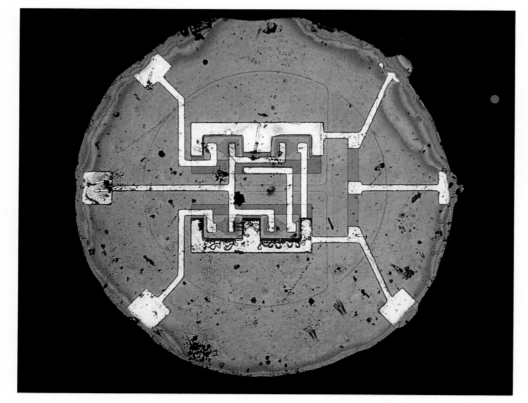

Spidery white aluminum leads link blue cone-shaped transistors and bar-shaped resistors on a tiny integrated circuit designed to perform logical operations in a computer. Chips like this one — shown enlarged about 60 times (the red patch represents actual size) — were first mass-produced by the revolutionary planar process in the early 1960s.

voltage applied to the base can act as a switch or amplifier for the main current.

The transistor could do everything the tube could do, but in a fraction of the space and with none of the tube's disadvantages: no fragile glass container, no filament that had to warm up, no overheating, no voracious consumption of power. Shockley's junction model would eventually gain dominance in the marketplace over the point-contact version, but the achievement of his colleagues, Bardeen and Brattain, was far from forgotten. In 1956, all three were recognized by their scientific peers when they shared the Nobel Prize in physics. (In 1972, Bardeen won a rare second Nobel for later research at the University of Illinois in the superconductivity of metals at extremely low temperatures.)

Although it was a prodigious scientific achievement, the transistor did not immediately sweep to commercial supremacy. Manufacturing difficulties kept prices high: The best transistors cost about eight dollars each, at a time when a vacuum tube cost 75 cents. Moreover, much additional research was needed before the device was thoroughly understood.

In the mid-1950s, however, the cost of the transistor was dramatically reduced. In 1954, Gordon Teal, a physicist who had moved from Bell to Texas Instruments, a newcomer to electronics manufacture, perfected a junction transistor made of silicon instead of germanium. Silicon, the main ingredient of ordinary sand, is the earth's second most abundant chemical element (second only to oxygen). Germanium, by contrast, is a rare element typically found only as a by-product of zinc refining and coal mining. Though the amount of germanium that went into a transistor was minuscule — less than $8/10,000$ of an ounce — it cost more than gold.

Improved production techniques cut costs even more. For example, researchers learned to grow large single crystals of silicon that were much purer than multicrystal blocks. (Silicon crystals are "grown" — built by accretion, rather like the way rock-candy sugar crystals are formed on a string.) They also found a method of adding the desired impurities that was both faster and more precise than the old way of dropping pellets into the silicon melt. The new diffusion method, as it was called, added dopants by a process of vaporization so exact that it was likened to adding a single grain of salt to 38 boxcarloads of sugar.

The decreasing cost of the transistor helped accelerate miniaturization in electronics — a trend encouraged by the military, which needed to cram complex electronic packages into missiles and other weapons, and also by the embryonic U.S. space program. This trend, in turn, led to several manufacturing advances.

Like vacuum tubes, transistors made by the existing method had to be hand-wired and -soldered together to form circuits. The process was tedious, and the resulting circuits occupied more space than proponents of miniaturization desired. Moreover, the components formed a little mound, or mesa, that protruded above the silicon and were thus subject to contamination and damage. Having to wire transistors together was doubly inefficient in view of the batch method by which they were manufactured: A number of transistors were etched simultaneously on a large wafer of silicon by means of a photoengraving process; they were then separated — only to be joined together later to make circuits.

A radical way to build smaller circuits, and to build them more cheaply, had been suggested as early as 1952 by G.W.A. Dummer, a British authority on radar. At a symposium in Washington, D.C., Dummer had proposed incorporating entire circuits — all the transistors, resistors and other components — in a single solid block of semiconductor material. As it happened, Dummer's own attempt to do just that failed. But an American engineer who had no knowledge of Dummer's work later developed the same theory — and made it work.

CREATING THE INTEGRATED CIRCUIT

Jack St. Clair Kilby was a six-foot-six-inch Kansan, a quiet introvert who had failed to get into MIT because his score on the mathematics entrance exam fell three points short of the required level. In May 1958, after a decade of working with transistors for a manufacturer of radio and television parts — the only company to offer him a job after he graduated from the University of Illinois — Kilby jumped at the chance to join Texas Instruments.

The fast-growing company, developer of the first commercially successful silicon transistor four years before, was then involved with a proposed miniaturization scheme for the U.S. Army. The idea, dubbed micromodules, was to print electronic components on tiny ceramic wafers and then wire them together in a stack to form a circuit.

Kilby regarded the plan as too complicated, and he began seeking an alternative. The solution came to him in July when the company shut down for a two-week vacation and Kilby, too new on the job to qualify for a summer holiday, found himself virtually alone in the lab. The key was Kilby's realization that not only could resistors and the charge-holding components called capacitors be made from the same semiconductor material as transistors, but these components could all be made simultaneously on the same piece of material — integrated on a single slice of semiconductor. A few months later he proved the concept to his skeptical boss by constructing a crude prototype.

The world's first integrated circuit — or IC, as such circuits came to be known — was a thin wafer of germanium two fifths of an inch long. The device was not elegant. Its five components were isolated electrically from one another mainly by shaping them into L's, U's and other configurations. The tiny wires linking the components to one another and to the power supply were simply soldered on, and the whole thing was held together by wax. But it worked. Texas Instruments announced its birth in January 1959. And to demonstrate its potential, the company built for the Air Force a computer that used 587 ICs; it occupied only 6.3 cubic inches, 1/150 the space taken up by the machine it replaced.

Such were the shortcomings of the new device, however, that Kilby soon found himself in the same position as John Bardeen and Walter Brattain, the inventors of the point-contact transistor. He got the patent and the richly deserved acclaim for being first, but his integrated circuit was quickly superseded by a version that was easier to manufacture.

Interestingly, the men responsible for developing the superior model were protégés of William Shockley, who had made the better transistor. Shockley had left Bell Labs in 1955, started his own semiconductor company near his hometown of Palo Alto and recruited promising researchers from the East. "He was very attractive to bright young people," recalled a colleague, "but hard as hell to work with." Two years later, eight of the brightest defected. They were fed up with such Shockley eccentricities as posting everyone's salary and requiring all employees to rate one another. The "traitorous eight," as Shockley called them, started their own company, Fairchild Semiconductor, only a dozen blocks away.

EN ROUTE TO A BETTER CIRCUIT

Within a year, in late 1958, one of the group made an important technological advance. Swiss-born physicist Jean Hoerni bettered the awkward mesa method of making transistors by finding a way to use thin coatings of silicon dioxide to insulate and protect the transistor's junctions. His method was called the planar process because the resulting transistor was flat, with no protruding mesa.

The planar process led to another giant stride forward — this one by Fairchild's director of research and development, 31-year-old Robert Noyce. Gregarious and athletic-looking, Noyce was the son of a small-town Iowa Congregational minister. Before going off to do graduate work at MIT, he had attended Grinnell College in his hometown. It happened to offer the world's first course in solid-state electronics, taught by an old associate of John Bardeen, who had sent him two of the first transistors ever made.

In Hoerni's planar process, Noyce saw clues for building an integrated circuit. About a month before Texas Instruments announced Jack Kilby's invention, he sketched out his own scheme in a lab notebook. "I'm lazy," Noyce explained later. "I invented the integrated circuit because I saw all these people putting wires on these gadgets and I thought it was terribly wasteful."

His working model, completed in 1959, had several key advantages over Kilby's version. For one, it incorporated breakthrough work done 3,000 miles away at Sprague Electric Company in Massachusetts by Kurt Lehovec. In April of that year, a few months after Kilby's achievement became known to the world, Lehovec had filed a patent for a "Multiple Semiconductor Assembly" whose components were separated from each other by p-n junctions, which let current flow in only one direction. Noyce's device combined p-n junctions with Hoerni's planar process and its silicon dioxide coating. To add wiring connections be-

Inside a Logic Gate

Every modern computer, no matter what its size or function, uses logic gates *(pages 42-43)* to carry out its work. Designed to react to electrical impulses in differing ways, logic gates enable the computer to perform a broad variety of tasks.

Whatever their type, all logic gates are made up of the same basic components, chiefly transistors — on-off switches capable of transferring an electric current or halting it. In NOT gates, transistors are arranged in such a fashion that a third operation becomes possible: The gate takes in a low-level signal and inverts it, sending out a high-level signal, and vice versa.

Shown here in schematic form are two transistors linked to make an AND gate. Such a gate passes current only if a high-level signal appears on all of its inputs. These signals, coming from other gates, switch on the transistors by allowing current to flow between the emitter and collector. The result is the continuation of current to another gate in the circuit.

Pictured in stylized cross section *(bottom)* and also in a bird's-eye view against the standard symbol for an AND gate *(below)*, a pair of transistors work in tandem to control passage of a supply current *(green arrow)*. Two independent high-level signals *(red arrows)* allow the transistors to conduct the current through the gate. Had either or both of these signals been low-level, the current would not have been able to continue.

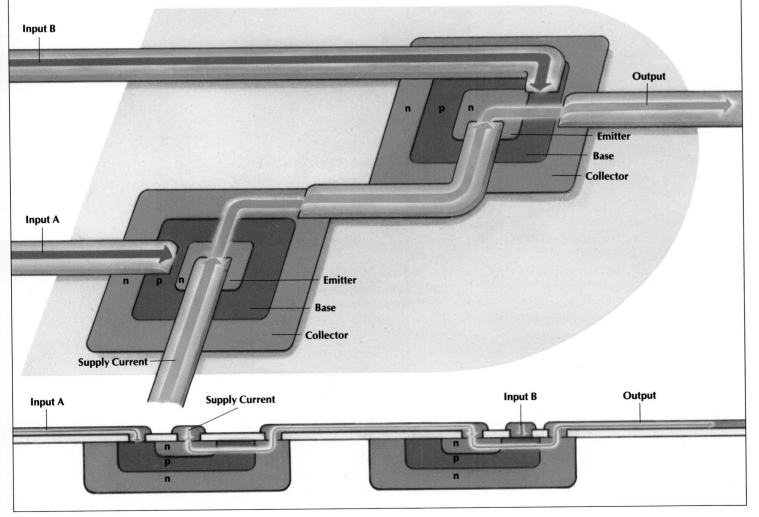

Input B

Output

Input A

n p n

Emitter

Base

Collector

Supply Current

n p n

Emitter

Base

Collector

Input A

Supply Current

Input B

Output

n
p
n

n
p
n

tween components, a layer of metal was evaporated on top of the coating and down into tiny holes etched in it—far more efficient than the conventional method of inserting minute wires by hand while peering through a microscope.

A RUNAWAY SUCCESS

The resulting IC was so much more practical than Kilby's that even Texas Instruments adopted it. In 1962, both Fairchild and TI began mass-producing ICs, which soon were nicknamed chips. Throughout the 1960s, as the size of each component on a chip shrank, the number of components incorporated there increased at a breathtaking rate, roughly doubling each year. In 1964, for example, a chip a tenth of an inch square contained a total of 10 transistors and other components. By 1970, no fewer than 1,000 components were crammed into the same-sized chip, at approximately the same cost as before.

Chips saved space, did away with the time-consuming need for wiring components together and, by minimizing connections, enhanced reliability. Just as important, they worked faster. Electric impulses darting from switch to switch at roughly half the speed of light now had to travel distances measured in mere hundred thousandths of an inch. The military and the space program embraced these tiny wonders wholeheartedly, building them into the controls of ever more sophisticated missiles and spacecraft.

The speed of the new chips was also crucial to the development of faster, smaller and more powerful computers for commercial and scientific applications. In the mid-1960s chips began to appear in this arena, first replacing computer logic circuits composed of discrete transistors, then supplanting so-called core memory, which stored information in the form of magnetic signals in an array of ferrite cores—tiny iron ringlets strung on wires.

The development of the computer memory chip was pioneered by a company called Intel—a name that telescoped the words "integrated electronics." The founders knew a lot about the subject—and well they might. They were Robert Noyce and two colleagues from the group of Shockley defectors that had started Fairchild Semiconductor. Intel in fact was only one of more than 50 companies that would be founded by former Fairchild employees, or "Fairchildren," as someone christened them.

In the now-familiar pattern, Intel set up shop near Palo Alto in 1968. Two years later, the firm introduced the first memory chip that could store an entire kilobit of information. (A kilobit consists of 1,024 bits, or binary units of information, the equivalent of about 25 five-letter words.) In the old magnetic-core memories, each core held one bit of information: a one or a zero, yes or no. Hence, the new Intel chip, which was less than a seventh of an inch long, replaced 1,024 cores that had occupied a space of about 80 square inches.

But a 34-year-old Intel engineer named Ted Hoff already was at work on a project that would prove even more remarkable. Marcian Edward Hoff Jr. had done advanced research in semiconductors at Stanford. He joined Intel soon after its founding because he "wanted to work on an idea with economic potential." Highly recommended by the Stanford faculty but modest and self-effacing, Hoff was actually Noyce's third choice for the job.

His project came from a Japanese manufacturer who wanted Intel to design a set of 12 chips for a new family of calculators. Such chips were always "hard-wired," permanently patterned so that the circuitry could perform only certain functions. Neither Intel nor Hoff had had much experience with them, which turned out to be a blessing. Looking at the problem from a fresh perspective, Hoff decided the proposed multichip system was much too complex to manufacture cheaply. Aided by Stanley Mazor, who joined Intel in 1969, and Federico Faggin, who arrived in 1970, Hoff came up with an ingenious alternative. He compressed the 12 chips to four, including a single processor that performed the arithmetic and logic functions of several chips. The processor held 2,250 transistors on a chip no bigger than the head of a tack. Moreover, it was not hard-wired. Its parts were arranged so that, like the central processor in a mainframe computer, it could be programmed to carry out almost any function desired.

Introduced late in 1971, this microprocessor was dubbed the 4004. Although it did not precisely live up to Intel's billing as a "computer on a chip," it came close. It contained all the functions of a computer's central processing unit. And when linked to as few as four other chips that contained memory, control and input-output circuitry, it yielded the microcomputer, an instrument as powerful as many mainframe computers of the mid-1950s.

THE ADVENT OF MOS TECHNOLOGY
Dozens of competing microprocessors soon appeared on the market, their development spurred by the resurgence of a technology that had been on the back burner for a while. In the early 1970s, the MOS transistor (for metal-oxide semiconductor) came into widespread use. Invented a decade before at RCA, the device has an extremely thin deposit of metal (later polysilicon) as its gate — the equivalent of the base in the junction transistor, which serves to switch the transistor on and off when a secondary voltage is applied. The MOS transistor

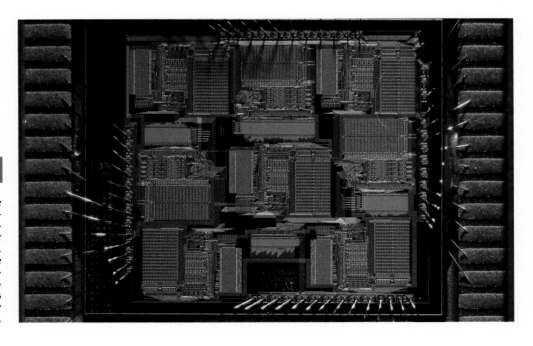

Bristling with no fewer than eight separate processors, this chip (whose actual size is represented by the red patch) is a prototype designed by scientists at Columbia University for a so-called non-von Neumann computer. "Non-von" computers operate on a principle called parallel processing: Instead of handling one piece of data at a time in a single central processing unit, many microprocessors work simultaneously with multiple data, vastly increasing the machine's speed and capacity.

made it possible to cram even more components on a chip and bring down prices precipitately. (By the end of the 1970s, some chips sold for less than five dollars apiece.) It not only was smaller and less expensive than the junction transistor but also consumed less power. This meant it generated less heat, a factor that had previously limited the density of integration. Circuitry consisting of up to 15 layers could now be emplaced in a chip $4/1,000$ of an inch thick.

Thus, by 1981, only a decade after Ted Hoff's invention, Hewlett-Packard could introduce a microprocessor *(page 103)* more powerful than the central processing units of many contemporary mainframe computers. Its speed—multiplying two 32-bit numbers in 1.8 millionths of a second—came from an array of 450,000 MOS transistors linked by 18 yards of vapor-deposited tungsten wire. All this occupied a silicon chip scarcely a quarter of an inch square, less space than a single transistor required before the invention of the integrated circuit.

Such remarkable shrinkage of components, known in the trade as very-large-scale integration, or VLSI, has been surpassed. In 1985, IBM began manufacturing memory chips arrayed with one million elements. Integrated circuits with 10 million components are on the horizon, and efforts are being directed toward the gigachip—an integrated circuit with one billion elements. In this realm engineers speak of ultrascale integration.

The obstacles to such an integrated circuit, though formidable, are thought to be surmountable. Design is one area of difficulty that is giving way. Computer assistance in mapping a microprocessor's circuitry was once limited to simulating the possible paths an electric impulse might take through the chip. Planning such a chip then took large teams of people as long as a year and a half, compared with the few weeks' effort required for the earliest chips. Engineering the gigachip under such conditions could easily be so expensive and time-consuming as to be impractical. Nowadays, however, computer software known as silicon compilers can—with ever-decreasing requirements for human intervention—translate a detailed description of a prospective chip's functions into a circuitry layout. This development clearly advances the day of the gigachip, as does progress toward engraving progressively finer details of circuitry through the use of X rays and electron beams in place of ordinary ultraviolet light.

Peering further ahead, many researchers envision far more radical approaches. Some suggest that new ceramic materials will permit computers to operate on photons, or light particles, instead of on electrons. Others, more daring still, look forward to the day when genetic engineers succeed in growing the "bio-chip," a chunk of organic material in which each of the billions of switches consists of a mere molecule of protein. Whatever the future holds in the way of chip technology, the developments since the mid-1960s have brought computers once and for all beyond the realm of big government and big business. The smaller and cheaper their innards became, the smaller and cheaper the machines themselves could be, opening the way to a truly electronic society.

Masterpieces of Miniaturization

Engineers formally christened it the integrated circuit, but virtually everyone — engineers included — calls it simply the chip. The more modest name fits its size if not its awesome capabilities: No larger than a fingernail — and often much smaller — this thin flake of a dull, metallic-looking substance called silicon can process or store information for almost any task imaginable, from operating computers, video games and home appliances to controlling robots on an assembly line.

Each modern chip is a layered puzzle of many hundreds of circuits so tiny they cannot be seen by the naked eye. The circuits consist in part of passive components such as resistors, which oppose the flow of electricity, and capacitors, which can store a charge. But the key elements are transistors, devices that can amplify a voltage or turn it on and off to speak the binary language of electronic information processing.

The many components in a chip are fashioned from the same underlying piece of silicon, a commonplace element that makes up 28 per cent of the earth's crust by weight. Silicon is ordinarily incapable of conducting electricity. But treating it with dopants — minute amounts of elements such as boron or phosphorus — subtly alters its crystalline structure, allowing the transmission of electrical impulses moving at half the speed of light.

Before the invention of the integrated circuit in 1959, each component of an electronic circuit had to be manufactured separately and then wired together. Chips changed all that, making electronics cheaper, more versatile, smaller, more reliable and—with less distance for electrical currents to travel—many times faster. Today's most advanced chips may hold a million or more components.

Fabricating a chip layer by layer involves photoengraving so precise that tolerances cannot exceed 4 millionths of an inch. This exotic and painstaking process, illustrated in part on the following pages, has created an entire new industry, projected to have annual worldwide revenues in excess of $180 billion by the year 2000. By that time, the electronics business as a whole, built on a chip foundation, will be far and away the largest industry in the world.

A Gridwork of Memory Cells

These three photographs, shot through a microscope, take progressively closer looks at the densely packed surface of a single read-and-write memory chip, which has been represented below at actual size *(red inset)*. Also known as a RAM chip, for random-access memory, it provides temporary storage for data while the computer is turned on; when power to the RAM is turned off, the data disappears.

This particular RAM chip contains more than 600,000 transistors and other components providing a net capacity of 256 kilobits, or 262,144 bits, of information — enough to hold an entire chapter of text from this book. Each bit is stored in an individual memory cell consisting of two electronic components: a capacitor, which keeps the data in the form of an electrical charge (representing binary one) or the absence of a charge (binary zero); and a transistor that

switches on to release the information or to allow a new bit to enter the empty cell.

The mass of 262,144 memory cells is divided into four equal sections *(below and top right)*. Within each of the rectangular quadrants, cells are arrayed in columns and rows. This arrangement, like the grid on a piece of graph paper, gives each cell its own coordinates. Locating the proper coordinates is a function of two bands of decoder circuits that bisect the chip horizontally and vertically. When ordered by the computer's central processor to find the address for a given byte, or eight bits, of information, the horizontal decoders locate the correct columns, and the vertical decoders pinpoint the proper rows. The entire operation — finding the cells and retrieving the byte of data — takes less than one millionth of a second.

A memory chip and a pencil point rest side by side, both magnified 14 times. The red inset reveals the chip's true dimensions — one quarter by one half inch.

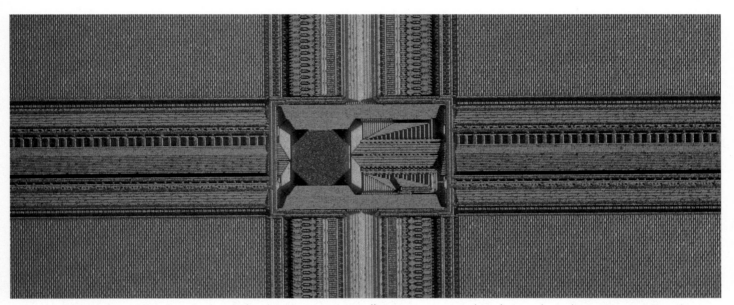

In this view of the chip's middle, where the decoder bands intersect, memory cells appear as mere specks in their quadrants despite 70-power magnification.

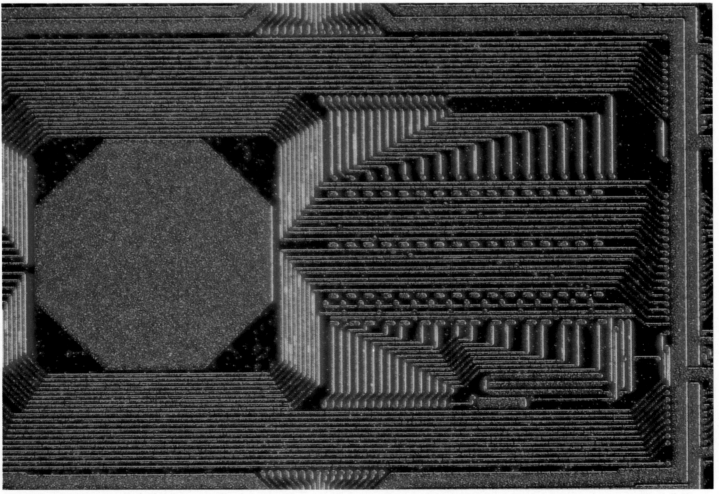

The central circuits in the decoder bands can be seen clearly at 300 times actual size. Colors stem from photographic lighting; the chip is actually dull silver.

A Range of Chip Functions

Though chips for computers come in many varieties *(box, opposite)*, the special functions of all of them can be combined to create a complete computer on a single device. The chip below is the TMS 1000, developed by Texas Instruments between 1971 and 1974; it was the first to bring together all the essential parts of a true computer. With its remarkable compression and low price—only six dollars in 1975—this so-called computer on a chip helped extend the power of microelectronics to such things as automobile dashboards, home appliances, telephones and juke boxes.

The version shown here was designed to operate a pocket calculator. A tour of its top reveals functions that, except in two cases, are usually found on separate chips. The read-only memory (ROM) *(1)* contains 1,024 bits of permanently stored instructions for operating the calculator. The read-and-write memory (RAM) *(2)* stores 256 bits of data needed only during operations. The control decoder *(3)* breaks down the instructions stored in ROM into detailed steps for action by the arithmetic logic unit (ALU) *(4)*, which actually carries out the numerical calculations; the ALU and control decoder together constitute the central processor, or microprocessor. The clock circuitry *(5)* connects the chip to an exterior quartz crystal whose vibrations coordinate the chip's operations, keeping everything in step. The input/output section *(6)* directs communications with devices on the outside of the calculator, such as the user keyboard and liquid crystal display.

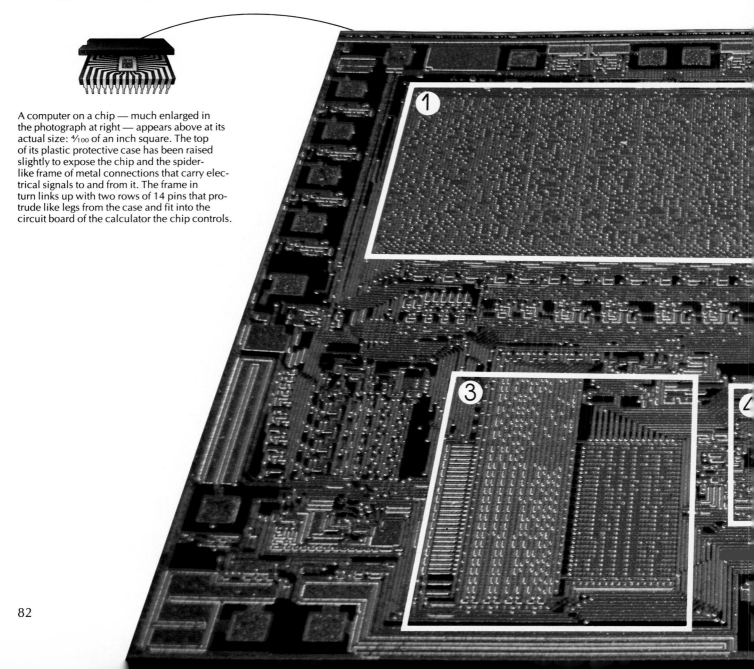

A computer on a chip — much enlarged in the photograph at right — appears above at its actual size: 4/100 of an inch square. The top of its plastic protective case has been raised slightly to expose the chip and the spider-like frame of metal connections that carry electrical signals to and from it. The frame in turn links up with two rows of 14 pins that protrude like legs from the case and fit into the circuit board of the calculator the chip controls.

Divisions of Labor

The typical home computer contains at least a half-dozen different chips. These are the principal types:

A clock chip monitors the regular pulse from a slice of quartz crystal that has been electrically stimulated and derives new pulses for use in other parts of the computer, synchronizing millions of split-second operations.

Interface chips translate incoming signals, such as the pressure of the user's fingers on the keyboard, into the on-off binary language of computer electronics. They also convert outgoing signals into data displayed on the computer screen as letters and numbers.

The microprocessor chip — the computer's nerve center — acts on instructions from programs stored in the memory chips to carry out all the calculations and logical decisions necessary in processing information. This work is done mainly in the chip's arithmetic logic unit, but the microprocessor also contains control circuits, which organize its work, and registers, which temporarily house data entering and leaving the chip.

ROM chips (read-only memory) hold permanent instructions for the microprocessor. Because these programs are imprinted on the chip during manufacture, they can only be read by the microprocessor chip, never changed.

PROM chips (programmable-read-only memory) provide various ways of updating or otherwise altering instructions ordinarily stored permanently in ROM. One type of PROM can be altered by ultraviolet light, another by electrical signals.

RAM chips (read-and-write memory) store data only as long as the microprocessor needs it for a particular operation. This data can be changed as well as read; new data entering the RAM cells automatically erases the old. Shutting off power also erases everything in RAM.

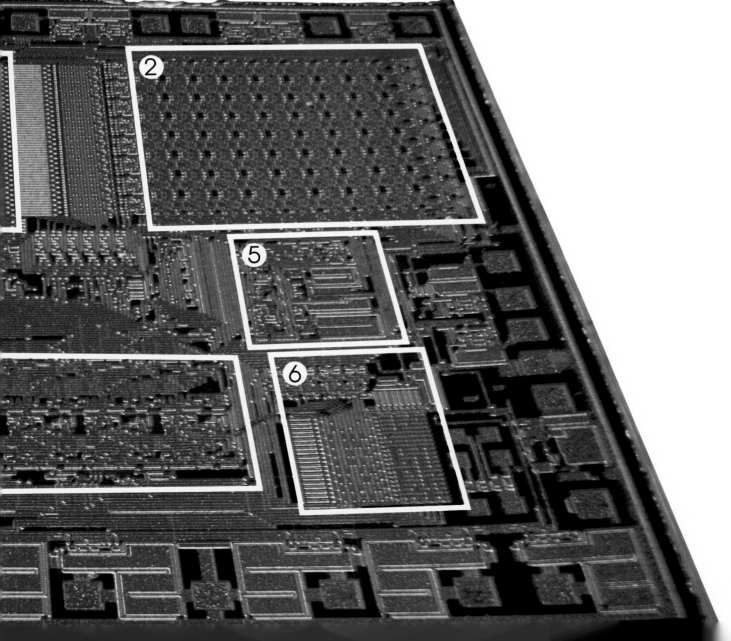

Designing the Pathways

Designing a chip demands extraordinary skill and patience—backed by help from a computer. For complicated integrated circuits, a designer usually resorts to a silicon compiler, complex software that enables the computer to do much of the work. But for a relatively simple chip like the one illustrated here, the designer may take a more direct hand in the process of chip design. Because a chip is fabricated layer by layer, its circuitry must be conceived in similar fashion, one tier at a

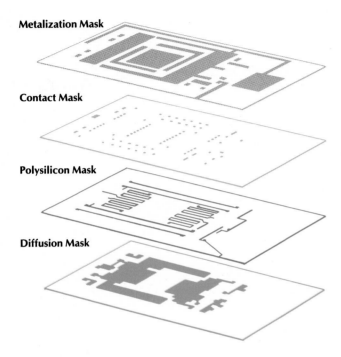

Metalization Mask

Contact Mask

Polysilicon Mask

Diffusion Mask

The photomasks shown above will make a simple four-layered chip for an amplifier circuit. Employed one at a time, the masks permit ultraviolet light to imprint the underlying chip with four separate patterns. Starting with the bottom mask, the patterns are used for: treating the chip with impurities to promote conductivity; depositing a layer of polysilicon to conduct the signal current; etching holes for metal contacts; and, finally, filling the holes with metal and then etching the excess to leave metal tracks to serve as connectors.

Seated at his computer, a chip designer studies two layers of circuitry, one superimposed upon the other. He faces a dual challenge: to find the most efficient routes for connecting all the circuits, and then to squeeze everything into the smallest area possible. The electronic pen in his hand enables him to arrange circuit patterns on a touch pad and see them displayed instantaneously on the screen. The computer records every component and its exact location in the planned chip.

time. Designers usually draw up a master plan for each layer with the aid of a computer, which can store standard circuit patterns and display alternative ways of linking them. Since the finished chip will be scarcely a quarter of an inch square, the drawings are done at a scale tens of thousands of times larger and then photographically reduced to the chip's intended size. The reduced pattern for each layer is reproduced on a glass plate to create a photomask. This mask, which acts like a photographic negative, allows light to imprint the pattern on the chip. The pattern defines the areas to be chemically coated, doped with impurities or beribboned with metal connectors.

To allow mass production of the chips, the pattern for each layer is repeated several hundred times across the surface of one glass plate. The photomasks for each layer are then applied in sequence to a single five-inch wafer of silicon.

As many as a million integrated circuits, or chips, can be made from an ingot of crystalline silicon two feet long and six inches in diameter *(left)*. Although silicon is a dull gray, the ingot's glassy surface here reflects the blue of its background.

Wafers only $4/1,000$ of an inch thick emerge from a fiery oven where heat sterilized their surfaces and polished any rough places left by the diamond saw that sliced them from the ingot.

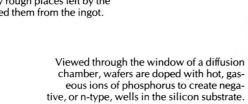

Viewed through the window of a diffusion chamber, wafers are doped with hot, gaseous ions of phosphorus to create negative, or n-type, wells in the silicon substrate.

From Ingot to Wafer

A chip-making facility seems more like a hospital than a factory, albeit a hospital touched with a stark beauty. Manufacturing is done in "clean rooms," places of near-absolute sterility in which even the air is scrubbed by special machines that filter out all foreign particles. Workers wear lint-free caps and smocks — and not a smudge of make-up. Pencils are banned as well, lest tiny bits of graphite flake off into the air.

The purpose of this obsessive cleanliness is to prevent contamination: A single speck of dust at any stage of manufacture can ruin a chip. Even the raw material must be pure. Silicon is refined from ordinary sand, then melted and grown — through a process that resembles dipping candles — into ingots *(top left)* that are 99.99999999 per cent pure. Wafers sliced from the ingots are baked to sterilize their surfaces *(bottom left)*. The only contamination allowed is that of doping the silicon with impurities to enable it to carry a current *(below)*.

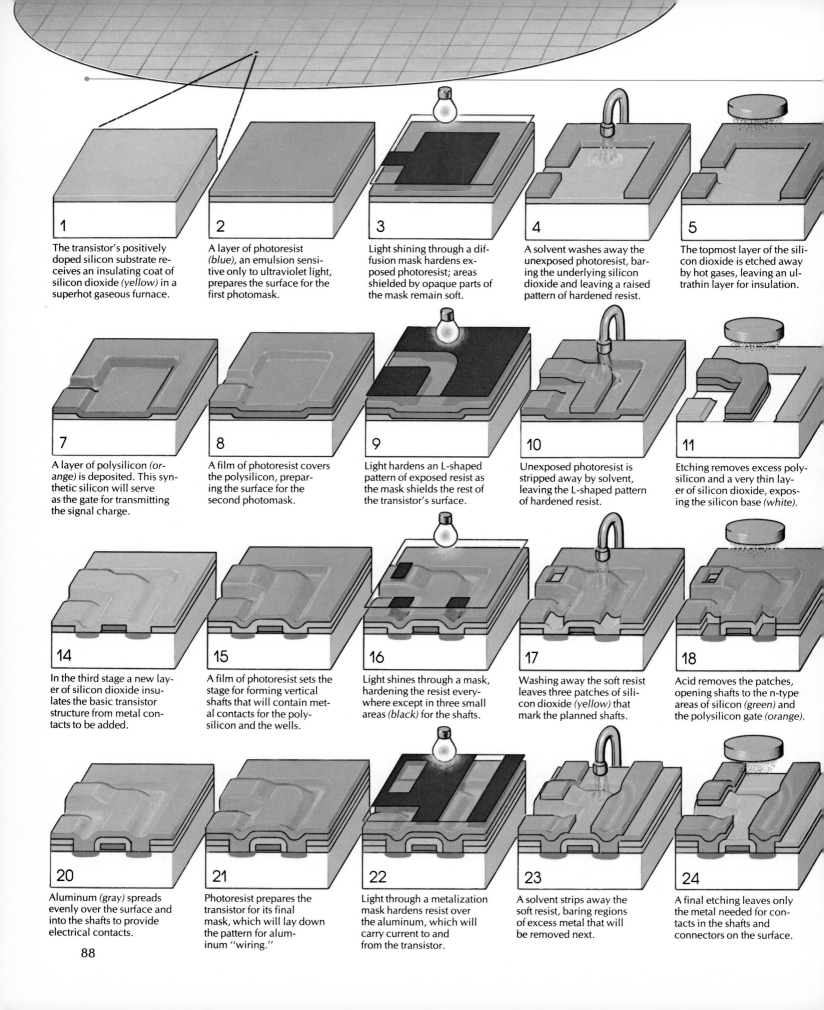

1 The transistor's positively doped silicon substrate receives an insulating coat of silicon dioxide *(yellow)* in a superhot gaseous furnace.

2 A layer of photoresist *(blue)*, an emulsion sensitive only to ultraviolet light, prepares the surface for the first photomask.

3 Light shining through a diffusion mask hardens exposed photoresist; areas shielded by opaque parts of the mask remain soft.

4 A solvent washes away the unexposed photoresist, baring the underlying silicon dioxide and leaving a raised pattern of hardened resist.

5 The topmost layer of the silicon dioxide is etched away by hot gases, leaving an ultrathin layer for insulation.

7 A layer of polysilicon *(orange)* is deposited. This synthetic silicon will serve as the gate for transmitting the signal charge.

8 A film of photoresist covers the polysilicon, preparing the surface for the second photomask.

9 Light hardens an L-shaped pattern of exposed resist as the mask shields the rest of the transistor's surface.

10 Unexposed photoresist is stripped away by solvent, leaving the L-shaped pattern of hardened resist.

11 Etching removes excess polysilicon and a very thin layer of silicon dioxide, exposing the silicon base *(white)*.

14 In the third stage a new layer of silicon dioxide insulates the basic transistor structure from metal contacts to be added.

15 A film of photoresist sets the stage for forming vertical shafts that will contain metal contacts for the polysilicon and the wells.

16 Light shines through a mask, hardening the resist everywhere except in three small areas *(black)* for the shafts.

17 Washing away the soft resist leaves three patches of silicon dioxide *(yellow)* that mark the planned shafts.

18 Acid removes the patches, opening shafts to the n-type areas of silicon *(green)* and the polysilicon gate *(orange)*.

20 Aluminum *(gray)* spreads evenly over the surface and into the shafts to provide electrical contacts.

21 Photoresist prepares the transistor for its final mask, which will lay down the pattern for aluminum "wiring."

22 Light through a metalization mask hardens resist over the aluminum, which will carry current to and from the transistor.

23 A solvent strips away the soft resist, baring regions of excess metal that will be removed next.

24 A final etching leaves only the metal needed for contacts in the shafts and connectors on the surface.

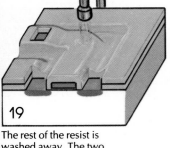

6

A chemical wash then removes the hardened photoresist to reveal an uneven surface of silicon dioxide.

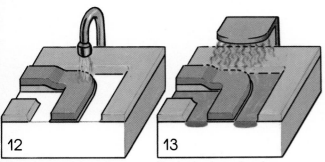

12

When the rest of the resist is removed, a ridge of polysilicon — the gate — rises above silicon wells.

13

Doping implants phosphorus in the wells, creating negatively charged areas *(green)* in the positively doped silicon.

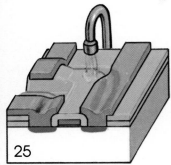

19

The rest of the resist is washed away. The two doped areas *(green)* will serve as source and drain.

25

The last resist is washed away and the transistor is finished — as are all the devices made with it on the wafer.

The Creation of a Transistor

The drawings at left illustrate in simplified form the step-by-step process of chip manufacture. In the actual process, which is immensely complex and can take up to two months, several hundred integrated circuits are fabricated simultaneously on a wafer of silicon like the one drawn at the top of the opposite page. Here, however, a single transistor — one minuscule part of one chip — has been enlarged about 2,500 times to stand in for the millions of parts and connections that are actually produced all together.

The process, called photolithography, begins with a $4/1,000$-of-an-inch-thick sliver of silicon that has been doped with impurities — in this example, boron, which creates "holes," areas of electron deficiency that act as positive charge carriers. In each of the four basic manufacturing stages (here represented by the four rows of images), this substrate of p-type silicon is coated with a thin film of photosensitive emulsion and then exposed to patterns of ultraviolet light projected through a mask. Various sequences of etching, doping, chemical coating and metal deposition create four layers, each scarcely $1/100$ as thick as the chip itself.

The completed transistor *(below)* belongs to a type called n-MOS, for negative-channel metal-oxide semiconductor. Because it is less power-hungry and generates less heat than the positive variety, it is used for applications that require cramming thousands of components onto a single chip.

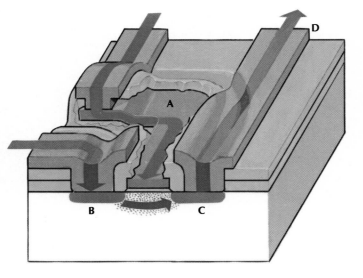

How the finished product works.
This cutaway drawing illustrates how the completed transistor operates as a switch. If no charge is applied to the polysilicon gate *(A)*, no current can flow from the n-type source *(B)* to the n-type drain *(C)*. But a positive charge *(red arrow)* applied to the gate acts across the ultrathin insulating layer of silicon dioxide *(yellow)* to create a temporary n-type channel, and turn the transistor on. Current *(blue arrow)* from the source can now flow to the drain. The current then exits through the aluminum connector *(D)* to other parts of the circuit.

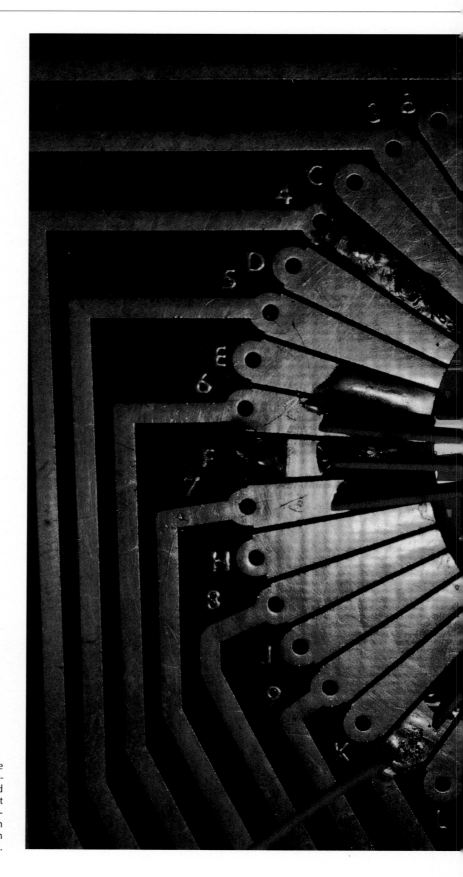

Newly completed chips — still part of the wafer on which they were fabricated *(center)* — are scanned by slender computerized probes. Up to 70 per cent of chips fail this first rigid testing procedure because of manufacturing errors or structural defects in the silicon itself. Defective chips are marked and then discarded after being cut from the wafer.

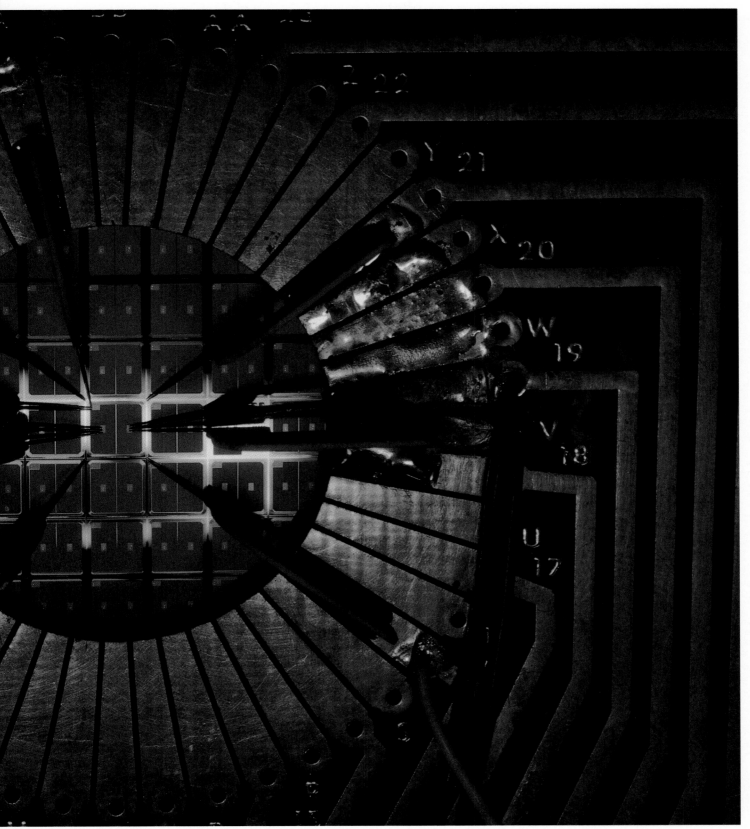

A Golden
Age of
Entrepreneurship

Between 1975 and 1981, computer technology changed so profoundly that those few years mark a watershed not just in the history of computers but in modern culture as a whole. Thanks to the silicon chip, the once-elephantine computer shrank in both size and cost until it was less elephant than rabbit, and it began to multiply and to expand its range accordingly. Along with that metamorphosis went equally significant changes in the attitudes and expectations that people brought to these machines.

In 1975, the idea of a personal computer — one owned and operated by a person rather than a large organization — was a dream cherished by few except hard-core electronics hobbyists. A manufacturer proposing to sell 800 build-your-own-computer kits by mail that year was considered absurdly optimistic by his bankers, who anticipated perhaps a quarter that many customers. Six years later, the outlook for small computers had altered beyond recognition. Fortunes amounting to hundreds of millions of dollars had been made (some only to be lost) by a collection of colorful and generally youthful entrepreneurs in the field. One manufacturer of personal computers astounded the financial community by rocketing onto the *Fortune 500,* a list of America's biggest businesses, faster than any other company in history: In its first half-decade Apple Computer grew from an almost assetless private partnership, consisting of two college dropouts assembling machines in a California garage, to a publicly traded corporation with a stock-market value in excess of a billion dollars.

In 1981, as the machines became familiar fixtures in classrooms, business offices and homes, personal computer sales hit the one million mark. Computer stores sprang up in every corner of the land, and newsstands bore the added weight of scores of computer magazines. Moreover, the personal computer industry had grown so big and profitable that it won over the cautious giant whose machines dominated the mainframe computer market. In 1981, IBM certified the technical, economic and cultural importance of the personal computer by announcing its intention to begin manufacturing its own desktop machine.

The story of this astonishing growth is one of technical wizardry, utopian vision and commercial daring. It is the story of a community of ''hackers,'' as computer enthusiasts call themselves, each longing for a computer of his own; of dreamers who saw in the computer revolution the world-transforming power they had hoped to find in politics, drugs, communes or religion during the 1960s and early 1970s; and of hard-driving, ambitious risk takers who believed that the dreams of hackers and revolutionaries could be given substance in a way that would enrich them all — and society as well.

Claiming their own personal computers — Altairs — ordinary citizens inaugurate a new age of computing freedom against a background of punched cards, magnetic tapes and paper print-out. This take-off on Socialist art — commissioned by the maker of the Altair — ran above the heading ''The People Computers'' on the cover of the December 1975 issue of *Interface* magazine.

Perhaps the greatest spur to the development of personal computing was the paradoxical blend of wonder and resentment inspired by the early large computers. Those electronic behemoths could perform marvelous feats, but because of their enormous expense and their fragility, they could function only in a carefully controlled environment, a world inaccessible to all but a chosen few. Isolated in specially air-conditioned rooms, tended by an elite corps of technicians — the "computer priesthood," as many users scornfully referred to it — these first- and second-generation machines were a source of deep frustration to many of the same people who found them most intriguing. Computer-obsessed students at such institutions as Stanford and MIT, craving hands-on contact with the technological objects of their desire, were forced to work through intermediaries, handing in programs coded on batches of punched cards, then waiting hours, often days, for the results. Like photographers barred from the darkroom or mechanics forbidden to look under the hood, they felt teased and cheated.

Minicomputers, a new class of machine arriving in the mid-1960s, changed the status quo only slightly. Although smaller and less expensive than their room-sized predecessors, minis were still large and costly by almost any other standard. Most of the early ones carried six-figure price tags and were big enough to fill a spacious closet. Minis were an important step forward, but they hardly represented the overthrow of the priesthood or the delivery of computer power into the hands of individuals. Only the microcomputer — the personal computer — would accomplish that.

However, the personal computer, while quick to conquer, was a long time coming. Just as there were assorted tinkerers trying out horseless-carriage designs before Henry Ford got into the automobile business, and many would-be aviators experimenting with flying machines before the Wright brothers flew at Kitty Hawk, so were there hundreds of electronics experimenters building their own primitive computing machines before the first commercially successful personal computer made its debut. Back in 1966, Stephen B. Gray, an editor for *Electronics* magazine, announced the formation of something called the Amateur Computer Society and attracted 110 initial members. Many were professional engineers who worked with computers owned by their employers and spent their spare time in garages and home workshops painstakingly constructing machines for their personal use. Yet it took another eight years before advances in microprocessor technology enabled a commercial product to hit the marketplace.

The new machine, the work of a Connecticut firm called Scelbi (for scientific, electronic and biological) Computer Consulting, was announced in the March 1974 issue of *QST,* a ham radio magazine. Scarcely four months later, the Scelbi-8H, as it was named, had its first competition: *Radio Electronics,* a magazine for experimenters, ran an article about the building of a machine called the Mark-8. Both the Scelbi-8H and the Mark-8 were based on the 8008 microprocessor chip from Intel. Despite the excitement they generated among electronics buffs at the time, they served as little more than curtain raisers to the main event.

That event began the week before Christmas in 1974, when the January 1975 issue of *Popular Electronics* (now *Computers & Electronics)* reached the newsstands. Featured on its cover was a machine billed as the "World's First Minicomputer Kit to Rival Commercial Models." Inside, the kit was offered for $397, and a fully assembled version of the machine for $498. "What we wanted for our readers," the magazine's editor wrote, "was a state-of-the-art minicomputer whose capabilities would match those of currently available units at a mere fraction of the cost."

THE ALTAIR FROM ALBUQUERQUE

Dubbed the Altair 8800, the machine was built around the Intel 8080, a more powerful descendant of the 8008, and it scored the first major success of what would soon become a multibillion-dollar industry. Like both the Scelbi-8H and the Mark-8, the Altair was not born in Silicon Valley, the familiar name for a stretch of western California between San Francisco and San Jose that would become a near-synonym for the semiconductor industry in the United States. Nor was it born in Cambridge, Massachusetts, home of the world-renowned computer scientists of Harvard and MIT. It came instead from the computer equivalent of nowhere — Albuquerque, New Mexico — and its creator was a burly, bespectacled young Air Force officer with a degree in electrical engineering.

Assigned to the Weapons Laboratory at Kirtland Air Force Base, Lieutenant H. Edward Roberts used his off-duty time to found a company he hoped would enable him to turn a profit from his lifelong fascination with electronic gadgetry. Roberts had built his first computer — a device composed of relays and stepping switches to control the valve on a heart-lung machine — when he was in his mid-teens. Earlier in his military career, while stationed in Texas, he had moonlighted as proprietor and sole employee of Reliance Engineering, a company that performed such services as designing the control equipment for an animated Christmas display in a San Antonio department store window. After his transfer to Albuquerque, Roberts got together with three buddies to establish a new company whose first products would be transistorized lights and radio transmitters sold by mail to model rocketry enthusiasts. They incorporated the new venture in 1969 and named it Micro Instrumentation and Telemetry Systems, hoping that the acronym MITS would confer something of the aura of scientific respectability enjoyed by the Massachusetts Institute of Technology, nearly 2,000 miles away.

MITS did not score an economic success with its line of model rocketry gear, or with such subsequent products as an infrared voice communicator and a laser kit. But these early efforts were not total losses. The voice communicator kit was featured on the cover of *Popular Electronics* as a so-called project article; that is, *PE* paid the designers of the device to write a piece about it for the magazine. Forrest Mims, one of the founders of MITS and an aspiring freelance writer, had been cultivating the relationship between the fledgling company and the magazine, and MITS projects were appearing with some regularity.

In 1971, MITS finally hit pay dirt with an electronic calculator kit, another *PE* cover story. The calculator was not a simple project. The design called for three separate printed circuit boards, a numeric key pad and a digital readout provided by electroluminescent display tubes built in Japan. It was the first large-scale integrated calculator kit produced in the United States, and it sold for only $179 (assembled, it cost $275). So successful was this product that in May 1972 Ed Roberts left the Air Force to devote himself to his mail-order calculator outfit. For a while the business thrived, and Roberts branched out into different types of calculators, intended mostly for hobbyists.

In 1973, MITS began selling assembled calculators to a retail company in wholesale lots of as many as 5,000 units a month. But by then, larger manufacturers had entered the market, offering calculators at cut-rate prices. It was no contest. That year, MITS sold $1.2 million worth of calculators — but spent $1.4 million to make them. "Once I got romanced into high volume," Roberts recalled a decade later, "it was hard to back up. Entrepreneurs are empire builders with giant egos. The mentality won't let you shrink until it's too late." Bankruptcy was on the horizon when he made one last gamble, leapfrogging calculators to develop something even more powerful: a small, affordable digital computer.

Exciting as the idea seems in hindsight, it might have fizzled without the catalyst supplied by *Popular Electronics*. After *Radio Electronics* — *PE's* archrival — ran the Mark-8 on its cover in July 1974, editorial director Arthur Salsberg decided to put a more powerful machine on *PE's* cover. Roberts' computer, designed around Intel's new 8080 microprocessor, was ideal. Salsberg assigned technical editor Leslie Solomon to oversee the project for the January 1975 issue.

Les Solomon was a playfully swashbuckling character, known for his quirky sense of fun and his penchant for spinning autobiographical tales that enthralled but did not always persuade his listeners. He talked about having fought along-

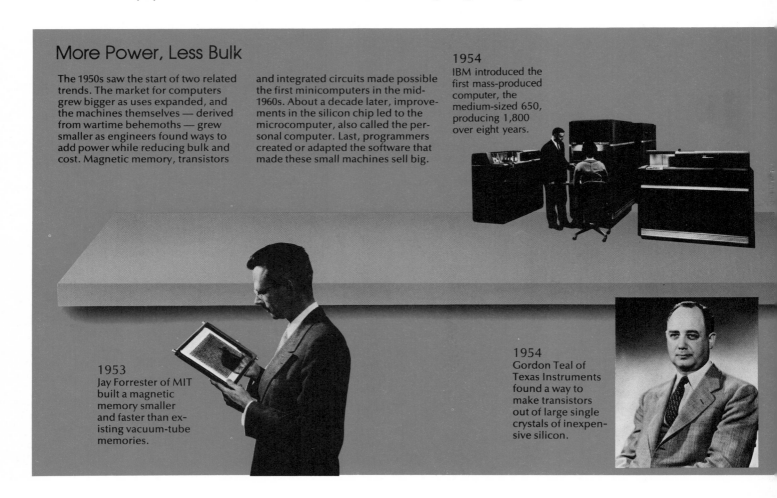

More Power, Less Bulk

The 1950s saw the start of two related trends. The market for computers grew bigger as uses expanded, and the machines themselves — derived from wartime behemoths — grew smaller as engineers found ways to add power while reducing bulk and cost. Magnetic memory, transistors and integrated circuits made possible the first minicomputers in the mid-1960s. About a decade later, improvements in the silicon chip led to the microcomputer, also called the personal computer. Last, programmers created or adapted the software that made these small machines sell big.

1954
IBM introduced the first mass-produced computer, the medium-sized 650, producing 1,800 over eight years.

1953
Jay Forrester of MIT built a magnetic memory smaller and faster than existing vacuum-tube memories.

1954
Gordon Teal of Texas Instruments found a way to make transistors out of large single crystals of inexpensive silicon.

side Menachem Begin for the creation of the state of Israel, and about journeys of spiritual discovery on which the holy men of Latin American Indian tribes had fed him hallucinogenic drugs and instructed him in mystical secrets. He claimed to be able to levitate weighty objects by mental energy alone.

After Roberts' machine had become part of industry folklore, Solomon told a story about the computer's naming that may be as apochryphal as it is appealing. In Solomon's version of events, he was casting about for something with more personality than PE-8, the name Roberts had chosen in honor of *Popular Electronics*. Solomon saw his 12-year-old daughter watching a rerun of *Star Trek* on television and thought it might be a good idea to name the MITS machine for the computer on the starship *Enterprise*. His daughter informed him that the spacecraft's computer was nameless, but suggested an alternative: Altair, after the star that was the craft's destination for that episode.

According to Forrest Mims, who wrote the Altair's operating manual, the mundane truth is that John McVeigh of the *Popular Electronics* editorial staff recommended naming the computer for a star in recognition of the fact that its introduction was a "stellar event." In either case, Roberts accepted the new

1958-1959
Robert Noyce, Jean Hoerni, Jack Kilby and Kurt Lehovec all took part in developing the integrated circuit.

1955
Bell Labs' first transistor computer, the TRADIC, held 700 transistors, each in its own container.

1961
Steven Hofstein devised the field-effect transistor used in MOS integrated circuits.

name for his computer distractedly, too worried about the possibility of going broke to spare much attention for such a trivial detail as what to call the machine.

To stave off bankruptcy while he prepared the first Altair for its appearance on the *PE* cover, Roberts had to seek a $65,000 bank loan. Much to his surprise and relief, his bankers granted it, in hopes of recouping the $250,000 they had already invested in MITS. Then disaster struck at the last moment: The one and only finished prototype of the Altair was lost by the shipping company en route from New Mexico to *PE's* office in New York City. With the printer's deadline approaching and no time to put together another computer, MITS and the magazine agreed in desperation to fake it.

The Altair that was photographed for *PE* was in reality an empty casing with no circuitry, no chips and thus no computing power inside. But it did what it was supposed to do. As soon as the magazine hit the stands, the fortunes of MITS experienced a startling upswing. With Intel selling the naked 8080 chip for $360, the Altair's $397 price tag was a steal (Roberts had earlier made a shrewd deal with Intel to buy the chips in bulk for about $75 each). Orders began flooding into Albuquerque faster than the little company could fill them. Roberts had barely

1965
Digital Equipment came out with the PDP-8, the first commercially successful minicomputer. Price: $20,000.

1971
Ted Hoff designed the Intel 4004 microprocessor — a single chip with all the basic parts of a central processor.

1968
Burroughs produced the B2500 and the B3500, among the earliest computers to use integrated circuits.

1974
Ed Roberts of MITS built a microcomputer called the Altair, which later sold as a mail-order kit for $397.

believed it himself when he told his bankers a short while before that he could sell 800 Altairs in a year, yet three months after announcing his personal computer to the world, he was struggling with a backlog of 4,000 orders. The machine, as one early buyer put it, "was an absolute, runaway, overnight, insane success."

That success spawned a host of enterprises that are now taken for granted in the personal computer industry. In July, a retail outlet, the first computer store in the country, opened in West Los Angeles to sell the Altair. One store became two, and eventually chains of computer stores materialized. Meanwhile, MITS vice president David Bunnell was editing *Computer Notes,* the first personal computer company newsletter; it was written for the company's employees but had an outside circulation of 12,000. A troop of MITS employees traversed the country in a van dubbed the MITS-MOBILE on an evangelical crusade to demonstrate the machine for new or prospective owners. Wherever the MITS-MOBILE went, computer clubs sprang into existence.

The enthusiasm MITS found in the marketplace was all the more remarkable in light of the Altair's rather drastic limitations. To save money, most buyers bought the kit version and had to assemble the computer themselves, a task requir-

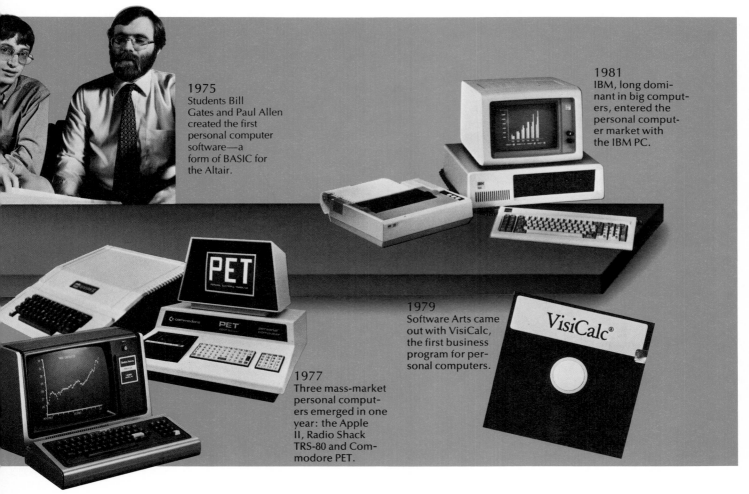

1975
Students Bill Gates and Paul Allen created the first personal computer software—a form of BASIC for the Altair.

1981
IBM, long dominant in big computers, entered the personal computer market with the IBM PC.

1979
Software Arts came out with VisiCalc, the first business program for personal computers.

1977
Three mass-market personal computers emerged in one year: the Apple II, Radio Shack TRS-80 and Commodore PET.

Engineer-entrepreneur George Morrow slyly reveals his new 8K memory board in this photograph for a 1979 advertisement. Morrow, who later made his own computer, sold the board as an add-on for the Altair.

ing no small amount of technical know-how if the finished product was to function properly. Even when expert hobbyists got their machines up and running, there was not much to do with them. The Altair could store only a thimbleful of data in its memory—256 bytes, compared with the several-hundred-thousand-byte memories routinely built into machines a decade later. Moreover, it had neither a keyboard nor a monitor screen: Users entered their programs and data in binary form by flipping a row of small toggle switches up or down, then read the result by deciphering the on-off patterns formed by the Altair's bank of flashing lights. MITS, struggling to stay abreast of orders, was slow to develop the software and attachments that would give the machine some real power and allow its users to progress from merely having a computer to doing some serious computing with it.

Fortunately for Roberts and his company, the joy of owning a computer, even one so rudimentary, seemed to be enough to keep the first wave of customers happy. People who would purchase a mail-order computer kit on the basis of an article in a magazine were not the type to quail before the technical challenges posed by the Altair. Hackers wrote their own programs for the machine and built their own add-on devices.

Ed Roberts had seen to it that the Altair was able to accept add-ons readily, just as the business-oriented minis could. He felt that the user should be able to install other functions simply by plugging in a circuit board. In order for the added boards to communicate with the main circuit board, however, the machine needed a system of buses, or wiring channels for data or instructions. The Altair's open-bus system — named the Altair-100 for its 100 wires — allowed the user to plug in up to 16 circuit cards for attachments and additional memory. The computer's blue and gray housing was built oversized to accommodate additional cards, and the power supply was designed accordingly.

Creating the bus was a rush job; there was no time for refinements such as eliminating cross talk, the electrical interference between wires packed too close together. But the do-it-yourselfers stuffed the Altair's cabinet to the bursting point. (The Altair-100 was later renamed the S-100 by competitors who used the design in their own machines; much to Roberts' chagrin, the new name caught on.)

THE CREATION OF AN INDUSTRY

Other hackers turned Altair-inspired creations into products for the unexpectedly large market Roberts had uncovered. Paul Allen, a young programmer in the Boston area, teamed up with Harvard student William Gates to write a version of a popular computing language called BASIC (Beginners All-Purpose Symbolic Instruction Code) for the Altair, giving the computer a language that made it easier for users to program their machines. When Allen flew to Albuquerque to demonstrate the product to Roberts, he was hired to run — in effect to create — the MITS software department. Later Gates and Allen would strike out on their own as founders of Microsoft, one of the most successful software companies in the personal computer industry. On the hardware front, a pair of students from Stanford designed a device that enabled the Altair to display color graphics on a television screen. Their company quickly expanded beyond Altair add-ons and in 1976 was manufacturing a rival brand of personal computer called the Z-2.

The Altair had touched a responsive chord in thousands of experimenters and hobbyists who longed to possess their own computers. Now the MITS success story stirred much larger dreams. From the dual motives that had driven Roberts to found MITS in the first place — a passion for technology combined with the desire to make a fortune — came the energies that formed an entire industry. By the time the Altair was a year old, more than two dozen manufacturers were active on the personal computer scene.

With the advent of the machines came other, related ventures. Publishers began producing magazines devoted exclusively to the subject of personal computing. Personal computer shows — starting with the First World Altair Computer Convention, held in Albuquerque in 1976 — provided a forum for the display of computer products and the exchange of ideas.

Unprepared for the voraciousness of the market and lacking the business acumen to back up its engineering expertise, MITS endured its headlong success for only two and a half years. In 1977 Roberts sold his still-thriving company to Pertec Computer Corporation, a firm that manufactured components for large computers. Pertec acquired MITS for $6.5 million in Pertec stock.

Roberts worked briefly for the new MITS owner, then left when the Pertec team of engineers pooh-poohed his design for a portable personal computer. "They were absolutely convinced that I didn't know the business," he said later. But even as he pursued a longtime dream of becoming a doctor, his entrepreneurial streak and fascination with electronics continued to bear fruit. In 1983, in a move that harked back to his earliest invention, he formed a new company to design low-cost electronic medical diagnostic tools.

The personal computer industry spawned by MITS and the Altair experienced its share of clashes and rivalries. Roberts himself had welcomed some manufacturers of add-on equipment for Altair users while railing against others he considered "parasites." For the most part, however, the companies born in the months following the Altair's appearance were more colleagues than competitors. The nature of the market encouraged an easygoing, cooperative style. Playful corporate names such as Kentucky Fried Computers or Itty Bitty Machines, and flowerchild names such as Loving Grace Cybernetics, proclaimed to the world that these companies did not see themselves as the traditional sort of earnest venture. Like MITS, all were serving a hobby market in which ideas and expertise were exchanged freely and enthusiasm for the magic of computing was stronger than the desire for economic conquest. If the *B* for business in IBM's name came before the *M* for machines, the priorities were reversed in the nascent realm of personal computing. Most of the early companies were like MITS — long on engineering know-how, short on marketing savvy.

BREAKING OUT OF THE HOBBYIST MOLD
The first personal computer maker to chart a more market-focused course was IMSAI Manufacturing, based in San Leandro, California. Headed by former IBM salesman William Millard, IMSAI — for Information Management Science Associates, Incorporated — made a concerted effort to give the personal computer a haircut and shoeshine and to introduce it to the business world. Scorning the hobbyist milieu that had given birth to the industry, IMSAI was determined to sell its small computers to the sort of corporate customers who would buy a lot of machines as serious office equipment, not as delightful toys.

The lighthearted cover of *Dr. Dobb's Journal* belies the magazine's wish to be a useful reference for computer hobbyists. First published in 1976 by the nonprofit People's Computer Company, the *Journal* offered advice, instruction and "calisthenics," or exercises, while carefully avoiding the "overbyte," or excessive demand upon computer memory, that would necessitate hardware "orthodontia."

DDJ

$2.00
In Canada $2.50

DR. DOBB'S JOURNAL of
COMPUTER
Calisthenics & Orthodontia
Running Light Without Overbyte

Number 45   May 1980   Volume 5, Issue 5

A REFERENCE JOURNAL FOR USERS OF HOME COMPUTERS
Special Issue!
The C Programming Language

A Small C Compiler for the 8080's
Ron Cain

The C Programming Language
D. M. Ritchie, S. C. Johnson, M. E. Lesk, B. W. Kernighan

Structured Programming, C and tiny c
Tom Gibson and Scott Guthery

Help with OSI's CP/M
Lee Barker

MITS DOS – Disk to Disk Copy Routine
Andrew Bender

An 8080 to Z80 Translator System
Robert W. Dea

PCC

Millard's aggressive, ambitious style was enhanced by his experiences with est, short for Erhard Seminars Training, one of the most commercially successful schemes to emerge from the era's so-called human potential movement. From the est program Millard learned to believe in his own invincibility, to deny the very possibility of failure. He filled IMSAI's top executive positions with others who had been through the est training and who shared his vision of the infinite possibilities open to those who maintained an unwavering faith in their own success. The phrase "make a miracle" became a semiofficial corporate motto, a frequently heard exhortation as IMSAI's managers set themselves dizzying sales goals and pushed relentlessly to achieve them.

And achieve they did. Formed shortly after Roberts introduced the Altair, IMSAI began shipping computers in late 1975; within a year the firm had vaulted to a position among the leaders of the infant industry. But even as sales skyrocketed, the company was heading for trouble. Push as it might, IMSAI's sales staff could not force the business world to embrace personal computers with true hobbyist fervor. Unlike the hackers who snapped up Altairs as fast as MITS could produce them, most executives cared nothing for the overthrow of the computer

A Gallery of Champions

Chip Name	INTEL 4004	INTEL 8080	MOS TECHNOLOGY 6502	MOTOROLA 68000
Date First Issued	1971	1974	1975	1979
Number of Components	2,250	4,500	4,300	68,000
Speed	adds two 4-bit numbers in 11 millionths of a second	adds two 8-bit numbers in 2.5 millionths of a second	adds two 8-bit numbers in a millionth of a second	adds two 16-bit numbers in 240 billionths of a second
Significance	the first microprocessor	the first microprocessor designed for general-purpose use; became the standard for the fledgling microcomputer industry	fast, powerful and cheap; widely used in popular home computers	one of the most powerful and versatile 16-bit chips; performs multiplication as a single operation rather than as repeated addition

The microprocessors in the table below are some of the most significant chips ever made. The first of them, the Intel 4004, which came out in 1971, was a four-bit device — a chip capable of processing four bits of information at once. Since then, the speed, complexity and processing power of chips have increased exponentially. In 1981 Hewlett-Packard produced the first of the 32-bit "superchips."

HEWLETT-PACKARD SUPERCHIP
1981
450,000
adds two 32-bit numbers in 55 billionths of a second
the first 32-bit microprocessor; so complex it took a team of engineers 18 months to design

priesthood or the joy of hands-on contact with chips, circuit boards and programming languages. They wanted to see the immediate practical benefit of the thing; and IMSAI's machines — almost direct copies of the Altair, albeit better designed in some respects — entered the market three years before a program called Visi-Calc, which enabled users to make financial projections, arrived to turn personal computers into serious business tools. Lacking useful programs, the company found its market limited primarily to electronics buffs with business ambitions.

Paradoxically, the other factor working against IMSAI's success was the very single-mindedness of its marketing orientation. Strong where the competition was weak, IMSAI also tended to be weak where the competition was strong. Other pioneers were in love with the technology and remained naïve, ignorant or just plain unconcerned about the ins and outs of sales and marketing strategy. The drive of Millard and his like-minded executives to achieve wonders on the sales front led them to shun IMSAI's engineering department, which was forced to keep pace with sales by rushing machines into production before their design had been properly tested.

That in itself was hardly fatal: Early buyers were used to temperamental, failure-prone machines. But they were also used to manufacturers who shared the hobbyist spirit and adopted a friendly, we're-all-in-this-together attitude toward solving problems and working out bugs. IMSAI's undisguised contempt for the world of hobby computing was not calculated to win the loyalty or affection of this community, much less of the many ordinary businessmen among IMSAI's customers. Following its rapid rise with an equally rapid fall, the company went bankrupt in 1979, about the same time Pertec phased out the MITS Altair.

A LANDMARK YEAR
Although neither MITS nor IMSAI had the necessary balance of engineering and marketing skills to sustain more than a brief ascendancy, three other aspirants did, and in 1977 all three entered the race. For the next two years, the two more established firms — Tandy Radio Shack and Commodore International — shared the lead in microcomputer sales. But an upstart company, the whimsically named Apple Computer, was hard on their heels.

Commodore was first off the blocks with its PET, for Personal Electronic Transactor, a computer announced in January 1977 (it was not actually available in stores until later that year). The company's founder was Jack Tramiel, an Auschwitz survivor who came to the United States as a teenager after World War II. Dynamic and demanding, he began his business career assembling typewriters and then progressed to manufacturing electronic calculators — some of the very machines that had helped drive Ed Roberts and MITS out of the calculator industry. In 1976, he plunged into a new field by buying out a small outfit called MOS Technology, whose founder, Chuck Peddle, had developed a chip called the 6502. With Peddle's know-how and the acquisition of another firm, Frontier Manufacturing, Tramiel was ready to take the microcomputer market by storm.

As it happened, another company had the same idea. Tandy Radio Shack was a Texas-based chain of stores that sold specialty electronics — kits and parts for devices ranging from citizens band radios to stereo equipment. The chain thus was in an excellent position to exploit the hobbyist yearning for personal computers. All it needed was a machine. In July 1976, the company recruited Steven

Leininger, an engineering graduate of Purdue University who was working at a Silicon Valley chip-making outfit called National Semiconductor. Over the next six months, Leininger and a small team labored in Radio Shack's Fort Worth headquarters to build a machine that could compete with the Altair.

During his sojourn in Silicon Valley, Leininger had moonlighted as a clerk at the Byte Shop, one of the first computer stores. Moreover, he had spent a lot of his spare time with the Homebrew Computer Club, a hacker's group whose influence on the new industry would be profound. In Leininger, Radio Shack had thus found someone who not only knew electrical engineering but also knew computer buffs. On his advice, the company scrapped its plan to sell computer kits and opted instead to develop a fully assembled model. Better yet, this model would let users do more than merely twiddle toggle switches and read blinking lights. Leininger, in a double feat not many could have pulled off, designed both the computer's architecture and its built-in software virtually singlehanded.

The TRS-80 Model 1 was built around the brand-new Z-80 microprocessor, closely related to the Intel 8080 but superior in performance. (The Z-80 was produced by Zilog, a company founded by former Intel engineers — a circumstance that led to legal wrangling later.) To give users an easy way to get data into and out of the machine, Leininger hooked it up to a television-like video monitor and a typewriter-like keyboard, adding a cassette recorder for permanent storage.

On February 2, 1977, after working around the clock for several days running, Leininger put the prototype through its paces for Charles Tandy, head of the company. Miraculously, everything worked. Blowing cigar smoke at the screen, Tandy allowed as how he liked the gadget. Someone asked how many they should build: 2,000? 2,500? The corporation's controller said, "We've got 3,500 company-owned stores. I think we can build that many. If nothing else, we can use them in the back room for accounting."

The Model 1 — the first microcomputer to be offered with components now taken for granted — went on sale that September. Ten thousand orders were placed in the first month, and demand remained so strong that the company's production line could not catch up for nearly a year. By the end of 1978, Tandy, blessed with a superb distribution system, had taken a clear lead over Commodore in the personal computer field.

The two-machine race was fast becoming a three-machine competition, however, as Apple got into the act. Formed as a shaky partnership in the spring of 1976, Apple underwhelmed the world with its first computer, the Apple I, only 200 of which were sold. But within a few years the company had come to dominate the market so completely and had cloaked itself in such a compelling mythology that many people took it for granted that the "two Steves," Stephen Wozniak and Steven Jobs, had founded an industry when they founded their firm.

APPLE'S ODD COUPLE

Wozniak and Jobs, whose success as entrepreneurs brought a kind of wildfire celebrity, were themselves a sort of MITS and IMSAI blend. They had little in common but electronics, the Los Altos, California, high school they had both attended and their friendship. Wozniak (Woz to his friends) was four years older than Jobs, who was all of 27 in 1983 when Apple appeared on the *Fortune 500* list. Woz was a conservative youth, censorious of the drug use so common

OUR FOUNDER

An original Apple I circuit board, playfully named Our Founder, was framed and hung in the company's first front office in 1977. Most of the roughly 200 Apple Is built were eventually traded in for Apple IIs.

among his contemporaries. His mother was active in Republican politics and once arranged for him to be photographed with California gubernatorial candidate Richard Nixon for the front page of a local newspaper. All through high school and his first try at college — one year at the University of Colorado, where he compiled an academic record larded with Fs — Wozniak was an archetypal computer "nerd," consumed by a devotion to technology that left little room in his life for such things as studying or social relationships.

For Jobs, on the other hand, computers and electronics were only one of many interests to be explored. His search for direction in life, for intellectual, emotional and spiritual stimulation, led him down assorted countercultural paths; he took drugs and experimented with a vegetarian diet, tried fasting, meditation and primal scream therapy, wrote poetry and fantasized about a literary career. He alarmed his parents by announcing that he intended to spend the summer after high school graduation living with his girl friend in a rented cabin. He dropped out of Reed College after one semester and worked at odd jobs for a while before returning to Los Altos. An interest in Eastern religions and mysticism then sent him to India a few times to visit temples, ashrams and religious festivals. When he finally set himself the task of creating and running a business, he tackled it with the evangelical fervor of someone who had at last found the meaning of life.

Wozniak, for whom there had never been any doubt that the meaning of life lay in computers, had a zany, prankish streak that contrasted with his seriousness about science. In fact, he often used his flair for electronics to further his career as a prankster. As a teenager, he once spent a night in juvenile hall for the crime of wiring up a fake bomb and planting it in a friend's high school locker. Later, he put together the equipment to run the original Dial-a-Joke from his apartment and, Polish-American himself, aroused the ire of Polish-American groups with the "Polack" jokes that made his the most popular telephone number in the San Francisco Bay area. Once, he devised a way to place a free telephone call to the

Vatican, mimicking Secretary of State Henry Kissinger and asking to speak with the Pope. His accent, not the technology, failed him, and he did not get through.

AT&T's computerized switching system held such fascination for Wozniak that he became an active member of the underground "phone phreak" culture. Phone phreaks were technological guerrillas, drunk with electronic exuberance or hostility to the corporate world, who crashed the telephone system for long and illegal joy rides through its network of cables, wires and satellite relays. The key was something called a blue box, an electronic device that emitted tones precisely calibrated to mimic the phone system's own equipment, thus fooling its computers and opening up long-distance circuits free of charge.

Some phone phreaks went to prison for their exploits. Wozniak went into business. It was his first enterprise with Jobs. Undaunted by potential legal repercussions, Wozniak built blue boxes while Jobs handled the purchase of parts and the sales of the finished product. Several years before they tried their hand at the lawful business of personal computers, the two Steves earned thousands of dollars supplying phone phreaks with expertly crafted electronic contraband.

Later, both went to work for prestigious firms in Silicon Valley. Jobs programmed video games for Atari, whose founder, an imaginative young businessman named Nolan Bushnell, was proving that millions of dollars could be made from computerized entertainment. Wozniak got a job as an engineer with the more sedate Hewlett-Packard. In 1975, when Jobs and Wozniak decided to build their own personal computer, the two young millionaires-to-be, with casual amorality, "liberated" parts for the machine from both employers.

HOMEBREW'S FERTILE ANARCHY

Wozniak, who did most of the design and construction, drew inspiration from the Homebrew Computer Club, from whose ranks would come more than 20 Silicon Valley entrepreneurs. The moving spirits behind Homebrew were a group of technology-minded activists who saw personal computing as an electronic means of delivering "power to the people." The moderator at the mildly anarchic meetings was Lee Felsenstein, an electrical engineer and one-time editor at the *Berkeley Barb* who later designed the first portable computer, the Osborne I. To Felsenstein, the personal computer revolution was a real revolution, a chance for individuals to seize control of a technology that had been hoarded until then by the Establishment. At Homebrew meetings, he promoted a cheerfully subversive atmosphere in which people traded equipment, ideas, even corporate secrets about cutting-edge research of interest to Homebrew hackers.

Wozniak reveled in the company of hobbyists whose enthusiasm for the technology was as keen as his own. Steve Leininger of Tandy Radio Shack remembered the meetings well: "Everybody looked more or less alike, in grungy jeans and beards. But there was a special aura — all these sparks going off." Woz called the Homebrew meetings "the most important thing in my life," and, encouraged and aided by Jobs, began work on a computer to show off at Homebrew meetings. It was not his first try at computer design; at the age of 13, he had won prizes at local and regional science fairs with a primitive arithmetic machine he called the Ten Bit Parallel Adder-Subtracter. In high school he and a friend constructed the Cream Soda Computer, named in honor of the soft drink they guzzled by the quart as they worked. Envisioning bold headlines and early fame, the boy genius-

Apple IIs roll down a production line in 1981, the year IBM entered the personal computer market. Much of the Apple II's success was due to its open design: The hardware and the operating system were not kept secret, allowing so-called third-party developers to write a variety of programs for the machine.

es staged a demonstration of their creation for a reporter and photographer from the same paper that had put Wozniak and Nixon on the front page a few years earlier. Their dreams of glory literally went up in smoke as the computer malfunctioned spectacularly for its media audience: A thick cloud billowed from its power supply and all its circuits ignominiously blew out together.

AN UNSPECTACULAR DEBUT

The machine Wozniak demonstrated at a Homebrew meeting in the fall of 1975 did not humiliate its maker, but it received a generally tepid response. So many enthusiasts were bringing in such makeshift devices that Woz and his machine did not really stand out. Only a few of his fellow hackers were intrigued by the clever use he had made of MOS Technology's new 6502 chip. Though less well known than the more fashionable Intel 8080 used in the Altair, the 6502 was — at $20 — also considerably less expensive. Woz shared the details of his design with the few who were interested and helped some of them to build their own versions of the machine. But it took Jobs to move the thing to market. He persuaded his friend to manufacture the computer for sale to Homebrewers and to some of the fledgling computer stores in the area. Then, in April 1976, the two signed an agreement officially recognizing their long-standing partnership. Apple Computer was born. (A third partner, Ron Wayne, who had been designated to write the operation manual, dropped out of the partnership after only a few months.)

As with Altair, the origin of the name Apple is a bit obscure. It was proposed by Jobs as an alternative to some of the harsher-sounding high-tech possibilities that were being tossed around along with the idea of the partnership. Jobs was much enamored of the Beatles and may have suggested the name of their recording company in homage to them. Or he may have been thinking of the All One Farm in Oregon, the commune where he had spent long hours working in the apple orchard after giving up on college. There was also a period, following his return from India, when he became a fruitarian and ate a lot of apples. In any case, Apple had the right organic and friendly sound for a company whose initial capital — $1,300 — was raised by the sale of a Volkswagen van and a fancy programmable calculator. "At least it got us ahead of Atari in the telephone book," Jobs said later.

Apple's first manufacturing facility was a spare bedroom in the Jobs family home. There, the two Steves assembled 50 machines for sale to the Byte Shop, the computer store that had employed Steve Leininger. As business grew, they relocated to the garage and continued their assembly work while Wozniak refined the design that would ultimately become the phenomenally successful Apple II.

That fall, Jobs and Wozniak received a visit at their garage headquarters from representatives of Jack Tramiel's Commodore International. Tramiel, who proposed to enter the personal computer market by buying out Apple, had sent Chuck Peddle and another Commodore employee to present an offer.

Apple and Commodore did not reach an agreement, but the sums of money discussed in their negotiations were dazzling compared with the modest profits from sales of the Apple I. Jobs began to think bigger and to look around for the money and talent that could help him design a company as exciting as Wozniak's machine. He sought out experts in the fields of public relations and venture capital, one of whom was A. C. "Mike" Markkula, a former Intel executive who had retired from the company a millionaire in his early thirties. Markkula visited the garage and liked what he saw in the combination of Wozniak's genius for design and Jobs's restless ambition. He invested some of his own money, effectively becoming a third partner in Apple, and used his industry contacts to attract more funding and executive talent. Markkula also supervised Apple's legal metamorphosis from a partnership to a corporation, a transformation that was consummated in the first week of 1977 — a little more than a year after Wozniak had carted his first Apple to Homebrew.

A 12-POUND SUPERSTAR

A few months later, the corporation's new product, the Apple II, was unveiled at the West Coast Computer Faire, a San Francisco trade show. Packaged in sleek plastic, it weighed just 12 pounds, could generate color graphics with a minimum of chips and possessed a sophistication — both as an engineering artifact and as a product for the mass market — that was unheard-of and unmistakable. In retrospect, the Apple II came to be regarded as the personal computer that catapulted the industry once and for all into the big time. The company's sales that year exploded to $2.7 million. Over the next few years, as pioneering firms like MITS and IMSAI dropped by the wayside, Apple continued its incredible growth. By 1980, when Apple wowed Wall Street with the biggest initial stock offering of any corporation since the Ford Motor Company, annual sales had reached $117 million.

Going public brought Jobs and Wozniak a combined fortune of nearly $400 million. The speed of their ascent to industry leadership and appearances on the covers of national magazines was the stuff of legend—with the Jobs family garage as a sort of 20th Century log cabin. Yet, even as Apple basked in success, the industry the company had helped to launch was nearing the end of an era that many, including the two Steves, were loath to see pass.

The following year IBM introduced the IBM PC, and with it a whole new age. IBM's entry into the fray erased any lingering doubts about the seriousness or the staying power of the personal computer, since it was taken for granted that Big Blue, as IBM was known in the trade, did nothing frivolous or frivolously. But IBM's presence also spelled doom for the home-brewed flavor, the informal hobbyist style that had enlivened the industry's earliest days. Once the domain of hackers to whom the world of big business was anathema, personal computing had itself become big business. Personal computing had been transformed by its rapid success, to be sure, but in the process it had irrevocably transformed the world. In the brief span between the Altair and the IBM PC, more lives were touched directly by computer technology than in all the years from Charles Babbage's first glimmerings of his Analytical Engine to the invention of the integrated circuit.

Of course, the PC and the Apple II turned out to be just a plateau in the rise of the personal computer. Before the end of the decade, such machines would more than triple in speed, then double again. They would shrink to briefcase size and smaller. Memory would grow by a factor of 10 and more, while disk storage capacity would jump from hundreds of thousands of bytes to hundreds of millions. Endowed with such power, personal computers have come to handle tasks that once yielded only to the brawn of a mainframe.

Anatomy of
a Lightning
Logician

Because they can do all sorts of complicated things — and do them at lightning speed — computers tend to inspire a certain awe in most novices. Examining a computer's electronics does little to explain its amazing powers. Yet, as spelled out on the following pages, the intrinsic structure and work methods of the machine are simplicity itself.

Each of the basic parts of a computing system *(page 110)* is assigned a specific task to be performed in a specific way. Two of those elements were first described in 1833 by Charles Babbage in his proposal for an Analytical Engine. Babbage postulated a "mill," where variables would be acted upon, and a "store," to hold those variables as well as the results of action by the mill. Today those elements are known as an arithmetic logic unit (ALU) and a memory, respectively. The ALU forms part of the computer's central processing unit, which carries out all instructions and regulates information coming in through input mechanisms such as a keyboard or a mouse, or going out to the user through output devices such as a printer or a video monitor.

All of a computer's various parts adhere to a mode of operation called serial processing. Whether the machine in question is a personal computer or a giant mainframe, it performs its tasks in an absolutely simple-minded step-by-step fashion, examining and acting upon only one instruction at a time before going on to the next. Even the smallest chore, such as adding two and two or changing a lower-case a to upper-case, involves completing hundreds of small routines. But each tiny step takes far less time than the blink of an eye, and after only a few seconds, the innumerable increments add up to a completed task that the user can appreciate, whether it be displaying an alphabetized list or shooting video-game invaders out of the sky. Pages 112-121 analyze a task that must precede all the rest — the actions a computer takes to ready itself for work.

An Overview of the System

The schematic drawings seen here and on the following pages explain the innards and the operations of a typical personal computer, but they are representative of virtually any computer system. Whatever the machine, it will have components similar to those shown below. A keyboard, for example, is the most common means of entering information and instructions; a video monitor and a print-

er are standard means of getting information back out to the user. And most systems will need the equivalent of a disk drive, a method of making permanent records or running additional software. All of these components plug into the system unit, which in turn houses the computer's electronic elements, arrayed on the system board shown on the opposite page.

The system board contains the central processing unit, or CPU, a microprocessor that directs the computer's activities. Every instruction must be examined and acted on by the CPU (sometimes by an auxiliary CPU) before it can be carried out. Another major player on the system board is a quartz crystal clock, which coordinates the responses of the computer's many circuits. When the machine is turned on, electric cur-

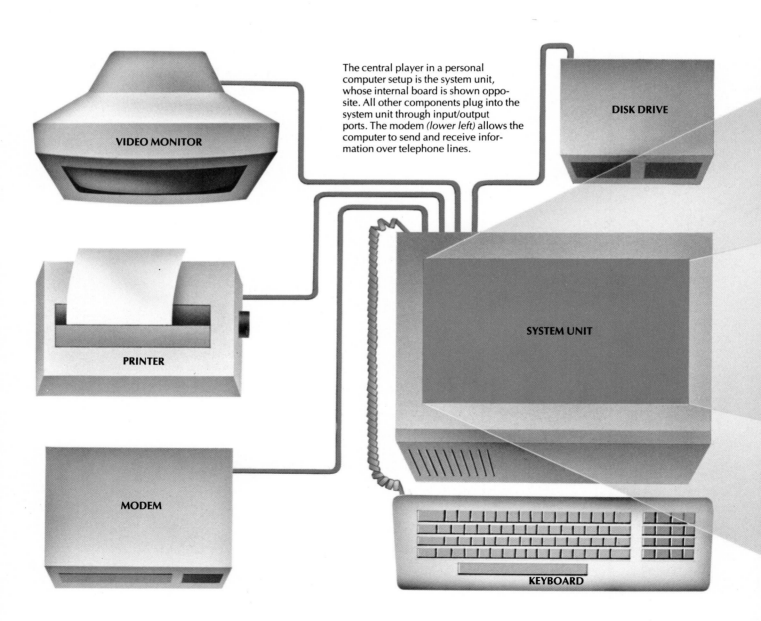

The central player in a personal computer setup is the system unit, whose internal board is shown opposite. All other components plug into the system unit through input/output ports. The modem (lower left) allows the computer to send and receive information over telephone lines.

VIDEO MONITOR

DISK DRIVE

PRINTER

SYSTEM UNIT

MODEM

KEYBOARD

rent causes the precisely cut sliver of quartz crystal to deform, or vibrate, at a constant rate — millions of times per second in some cases. With each vibration, the crystal emits a pulse of voltage. These regular pulses are combined with other signals to control the pace of action and ensure that the circuits do not get out of phase.

The system board also includes ports for connecting input and output attachments, and microchips for two types of internal memory: ROM, or read-only memory, and RAM, or read-and-write memory. (RAM originally stood for random-access memory, a misleading phrase no longer employed; but the acronym remains common usage.) ROM holds instructions that cannot be altered. RAM is used to store programs and information only while the computer is operating. The user can add to and change anything stored in RAM, but when power is turned off, RAM is wiped clean.

Each memory chip holds its information in the form of binary digits, or bits, encoded as electrical charges. These charges are stored at particular locations, or addresses, on each chip. Each address is also in binary form. Instructions go out from the CPU as a series of electrical pulses coded to find a particular address; the information found there returns — also as coded pulses — to the CPU for processing. Address codes travel on parallel wires called the address bus; information returns to the CPU on parallel data bus wires. The address decoder and the DIP switches (set to record certain important addresses) help direct the electrical pulses to their destinations.

Two key elements in a computer are the power supply, to convert alternating current to direct current, and the clock. Some clocks generate more than one set of pulses, allowing regulation of parts that operate at faster speeds.

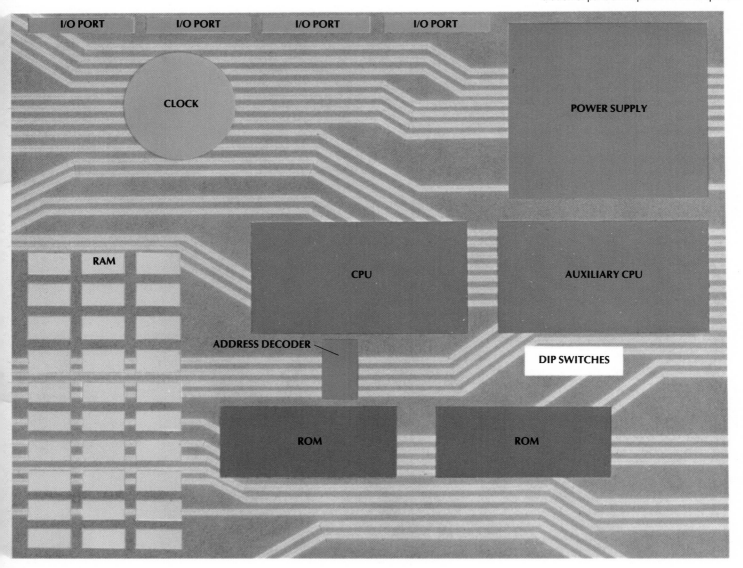

I/O PORT   I/O PORT   I/O PORT   I/O PORT

CLOCK

POWER SUPPLY

RAM

CPU

AUXILIARY CPU

ADDRESS DECODER

DIP SWITCHES

ROM

ROM

Triggering a Built-in Sequence

When the computer's power switch is turned on, electricity rushes through the entire system and a predetermined sequence of events begins. The quartz crystal clock starts sending signals out on the system's network at the rate of several million beats per second. Every action is regulated precisely by this rapid pulse, which is independent of the computer's other control signals. On the first beat of the clock, a reset signal automatically clears all the CPU's internal temporary storage circuits, or registers, of any random charges produced by voltage surges or left over from the computer's last use. In clearing a special register called the program counter, the signal resets the counter to zero *(opposite)*.

Now the machine is ready to carry out a process called bootstrapping (often shortened to booting) — so named because the computer, in effect, pulls itself up "by its own bootstraps." At the next beat of the clock, the program counter is loaded with an address that has been prepared for the system by the computer's designers; the address is usually set by adjusting so-called DIP switches *(opposite)*. The address — a sequence of high and low voltages expressed in this picture as the binary digits 11110010 — identifies the location in ROM of a start-up, or bootstrap, program. (For the sake of clarity, the address is shown as being only eight bits long; in reality, most microcomputers have addresses from 16 to 32 bits long.)

Bootstrap programs vary from one type of machine to the next. Sometimes the computer is directed immediately to check an external memory source such as a disk drive and to follow whatever instructions it finds. In the system illustrated here, the computer will check various internal parts of the system itself.

The CPU processes the start-up program in thousands of tiny steps; in this case, each step consists of one byte (eight binary digits). A byte may represent an address, or the instruction or piece of data found at a given address (a numeral, say, or a letter of the alphabet). Each byte travels as a sequence of high and low voltages on the address bus, represented here as a yellow band, or on the data bus, represented as a blue band.

As soon as the power is turned on *(top),* a host of actions take place so rapidly as to seem almost simultaneous. The first clock pulse triggers the reset signal, turning all registers in the program counter to zero. The program counter, which acts as a dispatcher, tells the CPU where to look for its next instruction. On the next beat of the clock *(right),* a prewired address pops up in the program counter. In this example, the address is for a location in ROM where the first instruction of a start-up program is permanently encoded. On the next clock pulse, the CPU copies the address (11110010) from the program counter onto the address bus *(yellow band).* By the end of the pulse, the next address in the sequence appears in the program counter.

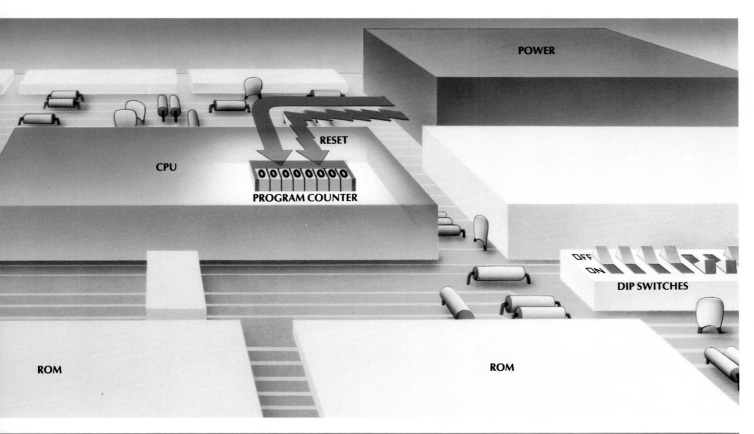

POWER

RESET

CPU

0 0 0 0 0 0 0 0

PROGRAM COUNTER

ROM

ROM

OFF
ON

DIP SWITCHES

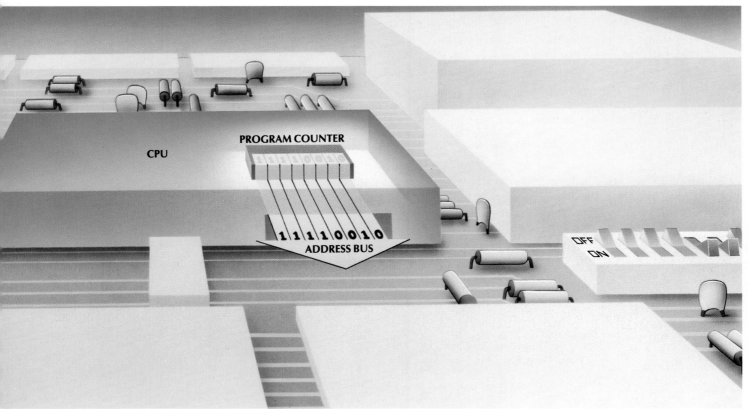

CPU

PROGRAM COUNTER

1 1 1 1 0 0 1 0

ADDRESS BUS

OFF
ON

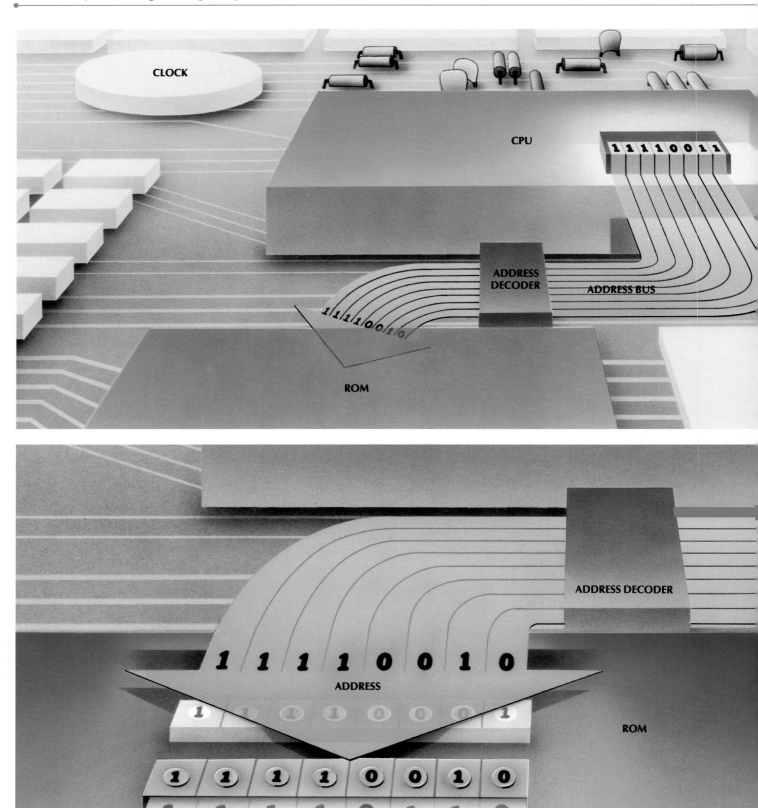

On a beat of the clock, the address bus latches, or secures, the eight-bit pattern of high and low voltages that represents the address of the first instruction of the bootstrap program. (The address of the next instruction is ready in the program counter.) On the following beat, circuits in the address decoder determine where the address is located. The next beat alerts the appropriate chip in ROM.

As the clock pulses on, circuitry inside ROM alerts the correct memory cells *(bright yellow circles)* in the selected chip. As shown here, the binary string representing the address is different from the string representing the contents stored at that address: An address refers only to the place where data is stored, not to the data itself. In this case, the eight-bit contents string is the binary encoding of the first instruction in the wake-up sequence. The CPU will want to "read" this information but must wait for a special signal and the clock pulse.

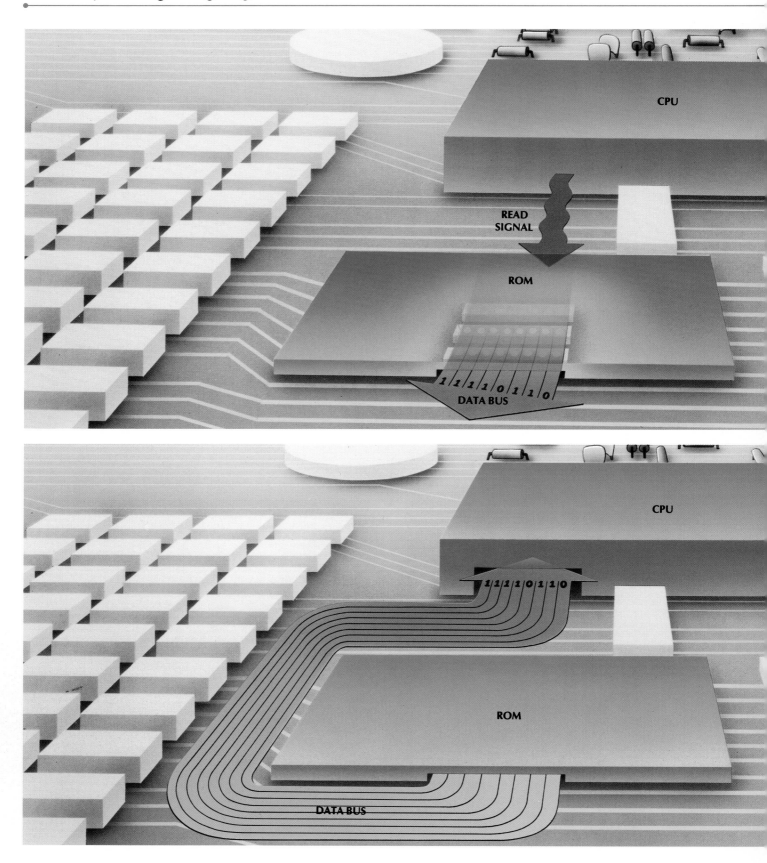

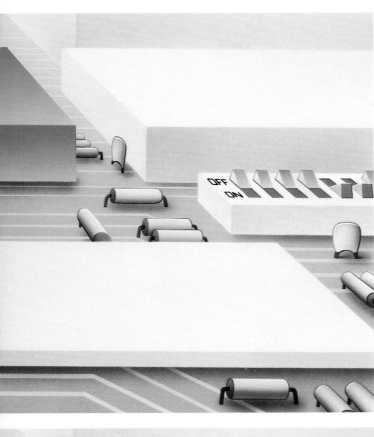

At the next beat of the clock, the CPU flashes the "read" signal to the ROM chip, which instantly transfers the data onto the data bus. This elaborate choreography of control signals and clock pulses is needed to ensure that nothing is sent out on the bus wires until a destination is ready to receive it. Routing the clock pulse and the "read" signal through a Boolean AND gate (page 75) prevents the data from being put on the data bus unless both pulse and signal are logically TRUE.

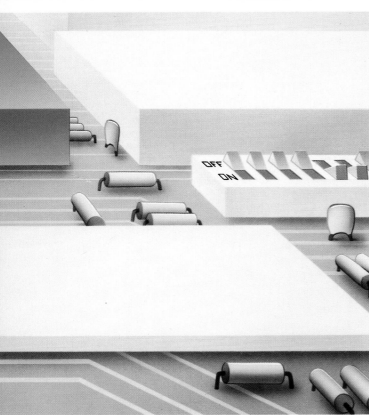

Once on the data bus, the byte of data selected from this initial address in ROM moves back to the CPU. On the next clock beat, the CPU latches the byte of data from the bus and sends it in to its registers. Since this is the first piece of data the CPU has received since the power was turned on, it interprets the data as an instruction to be decoded on the following beat of the clock. This sequence — program counter, address bus, ROM, data bus, instruction decoding — will be repeated hundreds of times, until all the bytes that go to form the wake-up instructions have been carried to the CPU, one by one, and executed.

A Multimillion-Step Check-out

The steps detailed on the preceding pages represent the kind of discrete actions that must be repeated over and over to get stored instructions to the CPU. Each of these actions occurs in the space of just a few nanoseconds (a nanosecond is a billionth of a second). What appears at right and on the next two pages is a larger view of the bootstrap program in operation—a view different in time scale but not in kind.

The routine illustrated at right shows the computer checking RAM, or read-and-write memory, to ensure the chips are in working order. The process is made up of millions of separate acts and, depending on the amount of memory in the computer, can take several seconds to complete. Checking RAM is a complex procedure for two reasons. First, a RAM chip typically holds up to 1,024 kilobits of information. (A kilobit is 1,024 bits—meaning that a single 64-kilobit chip, for example, can store 65,536 bits.) Second, these tiny, high-density chips store electronic information in a manner quite unlike the way it is stored in ROM. As illustrated on pages 114-117, the eight-bit unit of information the CPU read in ROM was kept on a single ROM chip. In RAM, the eight bits that make up a unit of data are held on eight different chips in a fixed sequence. This method allows the system designer to make the most efficient use of storage space and wiring in the system board.

To make sure there are no faulty chips in RAM, the CPU sends a test package of data on the address bus *(yellow)* to a given address. The address decoder alerts each of the eight chips that will hold one bit of the data, and the bits are stored in those chips. Next, the CPU asks to read the data it has just stored. The decoder must alert the eight chips to dispatch one bit each along the data bus *(blue)* to the CPU. The CPU checks the byte fetched from the chips against the byte it sent out; the two should be identical. To test a chip completely, the CPU must conduct this test once for each bit of the chip's capacity. Of course, in the process, seven other RAM chips will have been checked out as well. If the CPU finds errors, it may determine that certain sections of RAM are defective and should not be used.

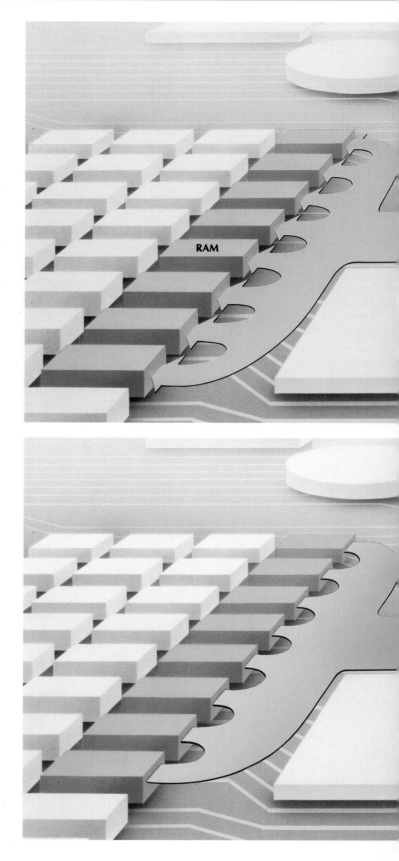

To test read-and-write memory, the CPU "writes," or sends, a sample piece of data to each location *(top)*. To write a byte of data to RAM, the address decoder seeks out eight separate chips, each of which stores one bit; together these eight chips make up one address. When the test data has been stored in RAM for a fraction of an instant, the CPU signals that it wants to read the data back into one of its registers *(right)*. The chips that contain one bit each of the sample byte release those bits onto the data bus. The byte is carried back to the CPU for comparison, and the cycle repeats until all read-and-write memory chips have been examined.

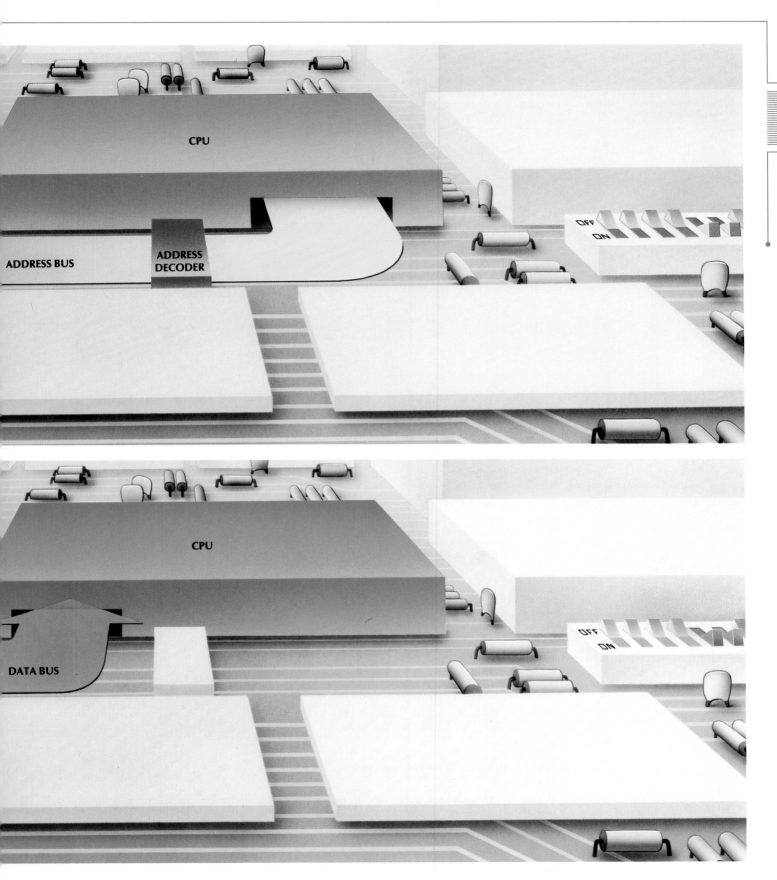

Anatomy of a Lightning Logician

After examining its bank of memory chips, the computer system shown here runs a similar check of its input and output (I/O) ports. The program controlling this activity is obtained, one instruction at a time, as on pages 112-119. The CPU now sends a series of repetitive signals to the ports along the rear panel of the system board. Ports for a monitor, a printer and other attachments are tested in turn.

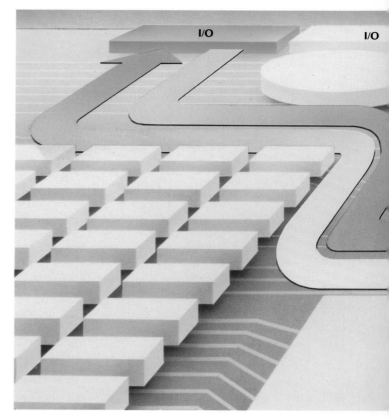

The last few instructions in the computer's bootstrap program tell the CPU to look in a special ROM chip to retrieve the next instruction. This chip contains a built-in language, usually BASIC, or a built-in user program, such as word processing. Only seconds after the power is turned on, control of the computer passes to this program or language. A message appears on the monitor to indicate that the computer is set for action. The message differs from one type of machine to another, but friendly greetings are common; here, an agreeable READY appears above a brightly lit cursor *(below)*.

READY.
>

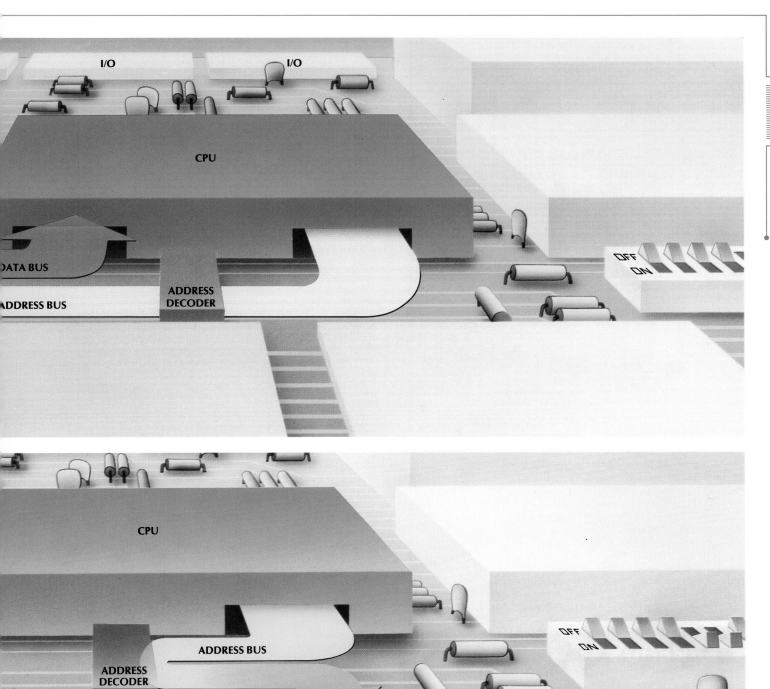

Glossary

Abacus: an ancient calculating device composed of a frame of rods, representing decimal columns, and beads that are moved on the rods to form digits.

Accumulator: a circuit in the central processing unit of a computer that can perform arithmetical or logical operations.

Adder: a circuit that performs addition.

Address: the location of a specific cell in a computer's memory.

Address bus: the wires in a computer that carry signals used to locate a given memory address; see bus.

Address decoder: circuitry that routes signals along an address bus to the appropriate memory cells or chips.

Alphanumeric: pertaining to the characters (letters, numerals, punctuation marks and signs) used by a computer.

Analog: the representation of a smoothly changing physical variable (temperature, for example) by another physical variable (such as the height of a column of mercury).

Analog computer: a computer in which continuous physical variables such as the movement of gears or the magnitude of voltage represent data.

AND gate: a logic circuit designed to compare TRUE-FALSE (or on-off or one-zero) inputs and pass a resultant TRUE signal only when all the inputs are TRUE; see logic gate.

Arithmetic logic unit: a part of the central processor that performs arithmetic operations such as subtraction and logical operations such as TRUE-FALSE comparisons.

ASCII: the acronym for American Standard Code for Information Interchange, a widely used system for encoding letters, numerals, punctuation marks and signs as binary numbers.

Binary: having two components or possible states.

Binary code: a system for representing things by combinations of two symbols, such as one and zero, TRUE and FALSE, or the presence or absence of voltage.

Binary number system: a number system that uses two as its base and expresses numbers as strings of zeros and ones.

Bit: the smallest unit of information in a computer, equivalent to a single zero or one. The word "bit" is a contraction of binary digit.

Boolean algebra: a method for expressing the logical relationships between entities such as propositions or on-off computer circuits; invented by the 19th Century English mathematician George Boole.

Bootstrap program: built-in instructions that take effect when a computer is turned on and prepare the computer for operation.

Bus: a set of wires for carrying signals around a computer.

Byte: a sequence of bits, usually eight, treated as a unit for computation or storage.

Capacitor: a device for storing an electric charge.

Carry: the digit added to the next column in an addition problem when the sum of the numbers in a column equals or exceeds the number base.

Central processing unit (CPU): the part of a computer that interprets and executes instructions. It is composed of an arithmetic logic unit, a control unit and a small amount of memory.

Chip: an integrated circuit on a fleck of silicon, made up of thousands of transistors and other electronic components.

Circuit: a closed network through which current can flow.

Circuit board: the plastic board on which electronic components are mounted.

Clock: a device, usually based on a quartz crystal, that gives off regular pulses used to coordinate a computer's operations.

Command: a statement, such as PRINT or COPY, that sets in motion a preprogrammed sequence of instructions to a computer.

Computer: a programmable machine that accepts, processes and displays data.

Control bus: the wires that carry timing and control pulses to all parts of a computer; see bus.

Control unit: the circuits in the CPU that sequence, interpret and carry out instructions.

Cursor: the movable spot of light that indicates a point of action or attention on a computer screen.

Data bus: the wires in a computer that carry data to and from memory locations; see bus.

Digit: a character position in a number (the number 344, for example, has three digits), or any one of the numerals from zero to nine.

Digital: pertaining to the representation or transmission of data by discrete signals.

Digital computer: a machine that operates on data expressed in discrete, or on-off, form rather than the continuous representation used in an analog computer.

Digitize: to represent data in digital, or discrete, form, or to convert an analog, or continuous, signal to such a form.

DIP switch: a series of toggle switches built into a dual-inline package (DIP) and used to encode various kinds of information, such as the amount of memory or the type of monitor in a computer system.

Disk: a round magnetized plate, usually made of plastic or metal, organized into concentric tracks and pie-shaped sectors for storing data.

Disk drive: the mechanism that rotates a storage disk and reads or records data.

Dopant: an impurity (most often boron or phosphorus) that is added to silicon for the purpose of enhancing certain electrical properties.

Electromechanical: composed of both electrical and mechanical, or moving, parts; most early computers were electromechanical devices.

Electronics: the science or use of electron-flow devices, such as vacuum tubes and transistors, with no moving parts.

Floppy disk: a small, flexible disk used to store information or instructions.

Full-adder: a circuit for adding two digits and a carry digit; see adder.

Gate: see logic gate.

Hacker: someone who loves to experiment with computers.

Half-adder: an electronic circuit that can add two digits but not a carry digit; see adder.

Hardware: the physical apparatus of a computer system.

Hard-wired: built in by the manufacturer and therefore incapable of being altered by programming.

Input: information fed into a computer or any part of a computer.

Input/output (I/O) port: an outlet on a computer circuit board for attaching input or output devices such as keyboards or printers.

Instruction: an elementary machine-language order to the central processing unit of a computer; a sequence of such instructions forms a program.

Integrated circuit (IC): an electronic circuit all of whose components are formed on a single piece of semiconductor material, usually silicon.

Inverter: a logic element that receives a single input and changes it to its opposite state.

Josephson junction: an experimental class of integrated circuit designed to operate at extremely high speeds (roughly one billionth of a second per operation) and at temperatures only a few degrees above absolute zero ($-459.7°$ F.).

Kilobyte (K byte): 1,024 bytes (1,024 being one K, or two to the 10th power); often used as a measure of memory capacity.

Language: a set of rules or conventions to describe a process to a computer.

Large-scale integration (LSI): the placement of 100 to 5,000 gate equivalents, or 1,000 to 16,000 bits of memory, on a single chip.

Liquid crystal display (LCD): a digital display mechanism made up of character-forming segments of a liquid crystal material sandwiched between polarizing and reflecting pieces of glass.

Logic gate: a circuit that accepts one or more than one input and always produces a single predictable output.

Machine language: a set of binary-code instructions capable of being understood by a computer without translation.

Mainframe computer: the largest type of computer, usually capable of serving many users simultaneously, with a processing speed about 100 times faster than that of a microcomputer.

Mask: a patterned plate used to shield sections of the silicon chip surface during the manufacture of integrated circuits.

Memory: the storage facilities of a computer; the term is applied only to internal storage as opposed to external storage, such as disks or tapes.

Memory chip: a chip whose components form thousands of cells, each holding a single bit of information.

Metal-oxide semiconductor (MOS): a technology for constructing integrated circuits with layers of conducting metal, semiconductor material and silicon dioxide as an insulator.

Microchip: a popular nickname for the integrated circuit chip.

Microcomputer: a desktop or portable computer, based on a microprocessor and meant for a single user; often called a home or personal computer.

Microprocessor: a single chip containing all the elements of a computer's central processing unit; sometimes called a computer on a chip.

Minicomputer: a midsized computer smaller than a mainframe and usually with much more memory than a microcomputer.

Modem: a device (modulator/demodulator) that enables data to be transmitted between computers, generally over telephone lines but sometimes on fiber-optic cable or radio frequencies.

Monitor: a television-like output device for displaying data.

MOS: *see* metal-oxide semiconductor

Nanosecond: a billionth of a second; a common unit of measure of computer operating speed.

Nibble: half a byte, or four bits.

NOT gate: *see* inverter.

Number crunching: the rapid processing of large quantities of numbers.

Operating system: a complex program used to control, assist or supervise all other programs that run on a computer system; known as DOS (disk operating system) to most microcomputer users.

OR gate: a circuit designed to compare binary TRUE-FALSE (or on-off or one-zero) inputs and pass a resultant TRUE signal if any input is TRUE.

Output: the data returned by a computer either directly to the user or to some form of storage.

Parallel: pertaining to data or instructions processed several bits at a time, rather than one bit at a time.

Ports: connectors for attaching peripherals to a computer's main board; *see* input/output ports.

Power supply: a device for converting external alternating current into the direct-current voltages needed to run a computer's electronic circuits.

Program: a sequence of detailed instructions for performing some operation or solving some problem by computer.

Program counter: a register that indicates the memory address of the next instruction in the program to be executed by the central processing unit.

Programmable: capable of responding to instructions and thus of performing a variety of tasks.

Quartz crystal: a thin slice of quartz that vibrates at a very steady frequency in response to an electrical current.

Random-access memory (RAM): a form of temporary internal storage whose contents can be retrieved and altered by the user; also called read-and-write memory.

Read: the process by which the central processor of a computer examines data in memory or transfers data to memory from an input medium such as a floppy disk.

Read-only memory (ROM): permanent internal memory containing data or operating instructions that cannot be altered in any way by the user.

Register: a special circuit in the central processing unit, such as an accumulator or program counter, that can either hold a value or perform some arithmetical or logical operation.

Relay: an electromagnetic switching device.

Reset: to return a central processing unit's registers to a zero state for a fresh start-up.

Resist: a material used to shield parts of a chip during etching.

Resistor: an electronic component that impedes the flow of current in an electronic circuit.

Semiconductor: a solid crystalline substance whose electrical conductivity falls between that of a metal and an insulator.

Serial: pertaining to data or instructions that are processed in sequence, one bit at a time, rather than in parallel (several bits at a time).

Silicon: an abundant semiconducting element from which computer chips are made.

Silicon Valley: an area of California south of San Francisco that is a center of the semiconductor industry in the United States.

Simulation: a computer program that manipulates the most significant variables in a problem or situation to show how a change in one variable affect the results; a re-creation of the situation by means of realistic sound and visual displays.

Software: instructions, or programs, that enable a computer to do useful work; contrasted with hardware, or the actual computer apparatus.

Solid-state: pertaining to electronic devices, such as transistors, made from silicon and other solid substances as opposed to vacuum tubes or electromechanical relays.

Tabulator: a machine that processes punched cards.

Teleprinter: a typewriter-like device capable of receiving or sending data in a communications system.

Terminal: a device composed of a keyboard for putting data into a computer and a video screen or printer for receiving data from the computer.

Transistor: a semiconductor device used as a switch or amplifier.

Vacuum tube: the earliest form of electronic switch, eventually replaced by the transistor.

Very-large-scale integration (VLSI): the placement of 5,000 or more gate equivalents or more than 16,000 bits of memory on a single chip.

Wafer: a thin, round slice of semiconductor material, usually silicon, on which hundreds of chips are made at once.

Word: the basic storage unit of a computer's operation; a sequence of bits—commonly from eight to 32—occupying a single storage location and processed as a unit by the computer.

Write: the process by which a computer records data in memory, external storage or display devices.

Bibliography

Books

Augarten, Stan:
  Bit by Bit. New York: Ticknor & Fields, 1984.
  State of the Art: A Photographic History of the Integrated Circuit. New York: Ticknor & Fields, 1983.
Chamberlin, Hal, *Musical Applications of Microprocessors.* Rochelle Park, N.J.: Hayden Book Company, 1980.
Davies, Helen, and M. Wharton, *Inside the Chip: How It Works and What It Can Do.* London: Usborne Publishing, 1983.
Ditlea, Steve, ed., *Digital Deli.* New York: Workman Publishing, 1984.
Eames, Charles, and Ray Eames, *A Computer Perspective.* Cambridge, Mass.: Harvard University Press, 1973.
Evans, Christopher, *The Making of the Micro: A History of the Computer.* New York: Van Nostrand Reinhold, 1981.
Fishman, Katharine Davis, *The Computer Establishment.* New York: McGraw-Hill, 1981.
Freiberger, Paul, and Michael Swaine, *Fire in the Valley: The Making of the Personal Computer.* Berkeley, Calif.: Osborne/McGraw-Hill, 1984.
Goldstine, Herman H., *The Computer from Pascal to von Neumann.* Princeton, N.J.: Princeton University Press, 1972.
Hanson, Dirk, *The New Alchemists: Silicon Valley and the Microelectronics Revolution.* Boston: Little, Brown, 1982.
Laurie, Peter, *The Joy of Computers.* Boston: Little, Brown, 1983.
Levy, Steven, *Hackers: Heroes of the Computer Revolution.* Garden City, N.Y.: Doubleday, Anchor Press, 1984.
Mabon, Prescott C., *Mission Communications: The Story of Bell Laboratories.* Murray Hill, N.J.: Bell Telephone Laboratories, 1976.
McWhorter, Gene, *Understanding Digital Electronics.* Dallas: Texas Instruments, 1978.
Mayall, W. E., *The Challenge of the Chip.* London: Her Majesty's Stationery Office, the Science Museum, 1980.
Mead, Carver, and Lynn Conway, *Introduction to VLSI Systems.* Reading, Mass.: Addison-Wesley, 1980.
Metropolis, N., J. Howlett and Gian-Carlo Rota, eds., *A History of Computing in the Twentieth Century: A Collection of Essays.* New York: Academic Press, 1980.
Moritz, Michael, *The Little Kingdom: The Private Story of Apple Computer.* New York: William Morrow, 1984.
Osborne, Adam, *An Introduction to Microcomputers.* Vol. 1, *Basic Concepts.* Berkeley, Calif.: Osborne/McGraw-Hill, 1976.
Osborne, Adam, and David Bunnell, *An Introduction to Microcomputers.* Vol. 0, *The Beginner's Book.* Berkeley, Calif.: Osborne/McGraw-Hill, 1982.
Randell, Brian, ed., *The Origins of Digital Computers: Selected Papers.* New York: Springer-Verlag, 1973.
Richman, Ellen, *The Random House Book of Computer Literacy.* New York: Random House, 1983.
Rodgers, William, *Think: A Biography of the Watsons and IBM.* New York: Stein and Day, 1969.
Rodwell, Peter, *The Personal Computer Handbook: A Complete Practical Guide to Choosing and Using your Micro.* Woodbury, N.Y.: Barron's, 1983.
Rogers, Everett M., and Judith K. Larsen, *Silicon Valley Fever: Growth of High-Technology Culture.* New York: Basic Books, 1984.
Shurkin, Joel, *Engines of the Mind: A History of the Computer.* New York: W. W. Norton, 1984.

Sobel, Robert, *I.B.M.: Colossus in Transition.* New York: Bantam Books, 1981.
Stern, Nancy, *From ENIAC to UNIVAC: An Appraisal of the Eckert-Mauchly Computers.* Bedford, Mass.: Digital Equipment Corporation, 1981.
Waite, Mitchell, and Michael Pardee, *Microcomputer Primer.* Indianapolis: Howard W. Sams, 1980.
Zientara, Marguerite, *The History of Computing: A Biographical Portrait of the Visionaries Who Shaped the Destiny of the Computer Industry.* Framingham, Mass.: CW Communications, 1981.

Periodicals

"America's Risk Takers." *Time,* February 15, 1982.
Bardeen, John, "To a Solid State." *Science 84,* November 1984.
Boraiko, Allen A., "The Chip: Electronic Mini-Marvel That Is Changing Your Life." *National Geographic,* October 1982.
Broad, William J., "Cosmic Rays Temporarily Disrupt Space Shuttle's Communications." *The New York Times,* October 9, 1984.
Clark, Wesley A., "From Electron Mobility to Logical Structure: A View of Integrated Circuits." *ACM Computing Surveys,* September 1980.
"The Computer Moves In." *Time,* January 3, 1983.
"The Computer Society." *Time,* February 20, 1978.
"Computer Software: The Magic inside the Machine." *Time,* April 16, 1984.
Creative Computing, November 1984.
Cromie, William J., and Harold A. Rodgers, "The Big Squeeze." *Technology Illustrated,* February/March 1982.
Davis, Monte, "The Chip at 35." *Personal Computing,* July 1983.
Evans, Christopher, "Micro Millennium." *Science Digest,* June 1981.
Guterl, Fred, ed., "In Pursuit of the One-Month Chip." *IEEE Spectrum,* September 1984.
Heath, F. G., "Origins of the Binary Code." *Scientific American,* August 1972.
Jones, Morton E., William C. Holton and Robert Stratton, "Semi-Conductors: The Key to Computational Plenty." *Proceedings of the IEEE,* December 1982.
Kilby, J. S., "Invention of the Integrated Circuit." *IEEE Transactions on Electron Devices,* July 1976.
Lund, Robert T., "Microprocessors and Productivity: Cashing In Our Chips." *Technology Review,* January 1981.
Martin, T. C., "The Electrical Engineer." *Scientific American,* August 30, 1890.
Mims, Forrest M., III:
  "The Altair Story." *Creative Computing,* November 1984.
  "The Tenth Anniversary of the Altair 8800: Setting the Record Straight." *Computers & Electronics,* January 1985.
Morrison, Philip, and Emily Morrison, "The Strange Life of Charles Babbage." *Scientific American,* April 1952.
Popular Computing, January 1985.
Posa, John G., "Superchips Face Design Challenge." *High Technology,* January 1983.
Reid, T. R., "The Chip." *Science 85,* January 1985.
Roberts, H. Edward:
  "The Industry: Where It's At!" *Personal Computing,* January 1985.
  "Starting an Industry." *Personal Computing,* November/December 1977.
Schadewald, Robert, "Devices That Count." *Technology Illustrated,* October/November 1984.
Scientific American, September 1977.

Shell, Ellen Ruppel, "Bach in Bits." *Technology Illustrated,* October/November 1984.

"Superchip Heralds A Revolution." *The New York Times,* July 3, 1984.

"Superconducting Chip Speeds Video Compression." *High Technology,* September/October 1982.

Toong, Hoo-min, and Amar Gupta, "Personal Computers." *Scientific American,* December 1982.

Walton, Marcus, "The Birth of an Industry." *Impact,* August 14, 1984.

Wolfe, Tom, "The Tinkerings of Robert Noyce." *Esquire,* December 1983.

Other Publications

Brotherton, M., "The Magic Crystal: How the Transistor Revolutionized Electronics." Bell Telephone Laboratories, Pub. No. PE-111, Revised October 1972.

Lustig, Lawrence K., ed., "Impact: A Compilation of Bell System Innovations in Science and Engineering." Bell Telephone Laboratories, 1981.

"Money Guide: Personal Computers." Time Inc., 1984.

Stevenson, Malcolm G., "Bell Labs: A Pioneer in Computing Technology." Bell Telephone Laboratories, 1974.

"Three Men Who Changed Our World." Bell Telephone Laboratories, 1972.

Acknowledgments

The index for this book was prepared by Mel Ingber. The editors also wish to thank: **In Great Britain: Harlow, Essex** — Paul Brierley. **In Japan: Tokyo** — Kodansha Ltd. **In the United States: Arizona** — Phoenix: Marshall Rothen, Motorola; California — Berkeley: Rodney Zaks, Sybex Books; Culver City: John Fries, West Coast Cycle; Salinas: John Pate and Art Romero, Radionics; Santa Clara: Michelle Davis, Intel Corporation; Margaret Harrison, Koala Technologies Corporation; Scotts Valley: Chuck Peddle; Sunnyvale: Margaret Woznick; Connecticut — Essex: Ted Flowers, Norelco; District of Columbia — Peggy Aldrich Kidwell, Museum of American History, Smithsonian Institution; Indiana — Kokomo: Robert H. Wathen, Delco Electronics; Michigan — Detroit: Pat Featherstone, Sheri Per-elli, J. A. Rosa and Chris Wallace, Cadillac Motor Car Division; New Jersey — Fairfield: Steve Eddy, Casio Inc.; New York — Garden City: Diane Fedyk and Sam Garcia, Nikon, Inc.; Les Solomon, *Computers & Electronics* magazine; Utah — Salt Lake City: Gregory McFarlane, Evans & Sutherland; Tennessee — Knoxville: Wayne Scott and Patricia Wilson, NAP Consumer Electronics Corporation; Texas — Dallas: Dick Perdue, Texas Instruments; Houston: Ernest Powell, Texas Instruments; San Marcos: Forrest M. Mims III; Vermont — Essex Junction: Irene Huluk, IBM; Virginia — Alexandria: David Page, Telemet America, Inc. **In West Germany: Hünfeld** — Dr. Konrad Zuse, Hannelore Zuse-Stöcker; Munich — Christel Glaser, Siemens-Museum; Dr. Rudolph Heinrich, Deutsches Museum.

Picture Credits

The sources for the illustrations that appear in this book are listed below. Credits from left to right are separated by semicolons, from top to bottom by dashes.

Cover: Larry Sherer. 6: Etsuo Genda, courtesy Kodansha Publishing Co., Tokyo. 8: Evans & Sutherland and Aerospace Corporation. 11: Trustees of the Science Museum, London, except bar, art by Matt McMullen. 12, 13: Trustees of the Science Museum, London (4); IBM except bar, art by Matt McMullen. 15-17: Art by James Hunt/Carol Chislovsky, Inc. 18, 19: Sam Garcia/Nikon Inc.; art by James Hunt/Carol Chislovsky, Inc. 20, 21: Art by James Hunt/Carol Chislovsky, Inc. 22, 23: Art by James Bandsuh from Nighthawk Studio/Carol Chislovsky, Inc.; Chrysler Corporation. 24, 25: Art by James Hunt/Carol Chislovsky, Inc. 26, 27: Art by James Bandsuh from Nighthawk Studio/Carol Chislovsky, Inc. 31: The Bettmann Archive. 32-35: Art by Greg Harlin from Stansbury, Ronsaville, Wood Inc. 48: Larry Sherer, courtesy National Museum of American History, Smithsonian Institution; Sony Corporation. 50, 51: Larry Sherer, courtesy National Museum of American History, Smithsonian Institution—Paul Donaldson, courtesy Cruft Photo Lab, Harvard University. 53: AP/Wide World. 54, 55: Courtesy The Royal Society, London; AT&T Bell Telephone Laboratories; British Crown Copyright, courtesy Brian Johnson, London—*The Boston Sunday Globe;* Alfred Eisenstaedt for *Life;* courtesy Professor Dr. Konrad Zuse, Hünfeld, West Germany; Leni Iselin for *Fortune* except bar, art by Matt McMullen. 56, 57: Marina V. N. Whitman; Smithsonian Institution; courtesy AT&T Bell Laboratories; Sperry Corporation—AP/Wide World except bar, art by Matt McMullen. 58: Art by Frederic F. Bigio from B-C Graphics. 63: Alan Richards, courtesy Herman H. Goldstine; art by Stansbury, Ronsaville, Wood Inc. 65 (computer): The Archives of the Computer Laboratory, Cambridge University. 66, 67: © Phillip A. Harrington/Peter Arnold, Inc. 68, 69: Art by Frederic F. Bigio from B-C Graphics. 71: Courtesy AT&T Bell Laboratories—Yale Joel for *Life.* 72: Courtesy Fairchild Camera and Instrument Corporation. 75: Art by Charles Williams. 77: © Phillip A. Harrington/Fran Heyl Associates. 79: © Phillip A. Harrington/Fran Heyl Associates. 80, 81: © Phillip A. Harrington/Fran Heyl Associates, courtesy of AT&T Technologies. 82, 83: Art by James Bandsuh from Nighthawk/Carol Chislovsky, Inc.; © Phillip A. Harrington/Fran Heyl Associates. 84, 85: Art by Charles Williams; © Dan McCoy/Rainbow. 86, 87: Motorola Inc.—© 1981 Harald Sund (2). 88, 89: Art by Charles Williams. 90, 91: © 1981 Harald Sund. 92: Forrest M. Mims III. 96, 97: IBM; Wayne Miller/Magnum (2); Texas Instruments; courtesy Kurt Lehovec, Ph.D.—The MIT Museum; courtesy Gordon Teal, Ph.D.; courtesy AT&T Bell Laboratories; RCA except bar, art by Matt McMullen. 98, 99: © 1980 Digital Equipment Corporation; © 1985, reprinted by permission of Intel Corporation; © William Thompson/Microsoft; IBM Archives—Burroughs Archives; © 1984 Forrest M. Mims III; Apple Computer, Inc.; Commodore Business Machines—Radio Shack, a Division of Tandy Corporation; Dan Cunningham except bar, art by Matt McMullen. 100: Herrington & Olson. 101: Library of Congress. 102, 103: © 1985, reprinted by permission of Intel Corporation (2); Dan Cunningham; Motorola, Inc.; Hewlett-Packard. 105: Apple Computer, Inc. 106: © Chuck O'Rear/Woodfin Camp. 109-121: Art by Matt McMullen.

Index

Time-Life Books Inc.
is a wholly owned subsidiary of
TIME INCORPORATED

Editor-in-Chief: Jason McManus
Chairman and Chief Executive Officer:
J. Richard Munro
President and Chief Operating Officer:
N. J. Nicholas, Jr.
Editorial Director: Richard B. Stolley

THE TIME INC. BOOK COMPANY

President and Chief Executive Officer: Kelso F. Sutton
President, Time Inc. Books Direct:
Christopher T. Linen

TIME-LIFE BOOKS INC.

EDITOR: George Constable
Executive Editor: Ellen Phillips
Director of Design: Louis Klein
Director of Editorial Resources: Phyllis K. Wise
Editorial Board: Russell B. Adams, Jr., Dale M. Brown,
Roberta Conlan, Thomas H. Flaherty, Lee Hassig, Jim
Hicks, Donia Ann Steele, Rosalind Stubenberg
Director of Photography and Research:
John Conrad Weiser

PRESIDENT: John M. Fahey, Jr.
Senior Vice Presidents: Robert M. DeSena, James L.
Mercer, Paul R. Stewart, Joseph J. Ward
Vice Presidents: Stephen L. Bair, Stephen L. Goldstein,
Juanita T. James, Andrew P. Kaplan, Carol Kaplan,
Susan J. Maruyama, Robert H. Smith
Supervisor of Quality Control: James King

PUBLISHER: Joseph J. Ward

Editorial Operations
Copy Chief: Diane Ullius
Production: Celia Beattie
Library: Louise D. Forstall

Correspondents: Elisabeth Kraemer-Singh (Bonn);
Christina Lieberman (New York); Maria Vincenza
Aloisi (Paris); Ann Natanson (Rome). Valuable assis-
tance was also provided by: Judy Aspinall, Vanessa
Kramer, Christine Hinze (London).

Library of Congress Cataloging-in-Publication Data

Computer basics.
  (Understanding computers)
  Bibliography: p.
  Includes index.
  1. Computers.   I. Time-Life Books.   II. Series.
QA76.C556 1989   004   89-5145
ISBN 0-8094-7550-2
ISBN 0-8094-7551-0 (lib. bdg.)

For information on and a full description of any Time-Life
Books series, please call 1-800-621-7026 or write:
Reader Information
Time-Life Customer Service
P.O. Box C-32068
Richmond, Virginia 23261-2068

UNDERSTANDING COMPUTERS

SERIES DIRECTOR: Roberta Conlan

Editorial Staff for *Computer Basics*
Designer: Ellen Robling
Associate Editor: Robert G. Mason (pictures)
Series Coordinator: Caroline A. Boubin

Researchers:
Elise Ritter Gibson
Sara Mark
Barbara Moir
Marta A. Sanchez
Judith W. Shanks

Text Editors:
Russell B. Adams, Jr.
Donald Davison
Cantlay

Assistant Designer: Robert K. Herndon
Copy Coordinator: Anthony K. Pordes
Picture Coordinator: Renée DeSandies

Special Contributors (text): Ronald H. Bailey,
Sarah Brash, Michael Kurland, Charles C. Smith,
Marlene Zimmerman

THE CONSULTANTS

ISABEL LIDA NIRENBERG has worked on a wide range
of computer applications, from the analysis of data collected by the Pioneer space probes to the matching of
children and families for adoption agencies. She manages
the computer system at the State University of New York
at Albany, and assists faculty and students there with
microcomputer applications.

UTA C. MERZBACH, a mathematician trained in the
history of science, has served as the Curator of the mathematical and computing collections of the Smithsonian
Institution's National Museum of American History since
1963.

RICHARD MURRAY is an Assistant Professor of Computer Science at Union College in Schenectady, New
York. He has also worked in the computer industry as a
software developer and product manager. His area of
research is VLSI (very-large-scale-integration) testing.

REVISIONS STAFF

EDITOR: Lee Hassig

Writer: Esther Ferington
Designer: Lorraine D. Rivard
Copy Coordinator: Anne Farr
Picture Coordinator: Robert H. Wooldridge, Jr.

Consultant: Michael R. Williams, a professor of computer science at the University of Calgary in Canada,
is the author of *A History of Computing Technology*.